The Perversity of Gratitude

GRANT FARRED

The Perversity of Gratitude

An Apartheid Education

TEMPLE UNIVERSITY PRESS 丅 *Philadelphia / Rome / Tokyo*

TEMPLE UNIVERSITY PRESS
Philadelphia, Pennsylvania 19122
tupress.temple.edu

Library of Congress Cataloging-in-Publication Data

Names: Farred, Grant, author.
Title: The perversity of gratitude : an apartheid education / Grant Farred.
Description: Philadelphia : Temple University Press, 2024. | Includes
index. | Summary: "While recollecting his educational experiences in
apartheid South Africa, the author grapples with the oppressive intent
of the governing regime alongside its unintended benefits for his
intellectual and individual development"— Provided by publisher.
Identifiers: LCCN 2023025392 (print) | LCCN 2023025393 (ebook) | ISBN
9781439924969 (cloth) | ISBN 9781439924976 (paperback) | ISBN
9781439924983 (pdf)
Subjects: LCSH: Farred, Grant. | College teachers—Biography. | Gratitude.
| Thought and thinking. | Apartheid—South Africa—Psychological
aspects. | Black people—Education—South Africa. | Education—South
Africa—Biography.
Classification: LCC LB1778.4.S62 F37 2024 (print) | LCC LB1778.4.S62
(ebook) | DDC 378.1/20968—dc23/eng/20230818
LC record available at https://lccn.loc.gov/2023025392
LC ebook record available at https://lccn.loc.gov/2023025393

This book is dedicated to the intellectuals

who were my teachers.

I pay tribute here to these teachers who remain,

indefatigably, the first models of the intellectual

whom I encountered:

Richard Owen Dudley: April 15, 1924–May 31, 2009

Morgan MacArthur: September 13, 1942–

Stanley Gordon Moysey Ridge: July 1, 1942–January 30, 2018

Richard Moore Rive: March 1, 1931–June 4, 1989

It is impassable, *indisputable*: I cannot challenge it except by testifying to its omnipresence in me. It would always have preceded me. It is me. (Derrida's italics)

—Jacques Derrida,

Monolingualism of the Other Or the Prosthesis of Origin

Contents

Preface

Thinking/Denke

Apartheid made me think.

Apartheid made me think, and, as such, my apartheid education constituted the optimal conditions for thinking. Truer still, it would be possible to say that apartheid, because of how it was conceived as a political system, provided the optimal conditions for disenfranchised thinking. The strict implementation of racial segregation in every facet of South African life—which school one could attend, in which train carriage one could travel, at which hospital entrance one was admitted—made thinking apartheid imperative. Apartheid demanded that the disenfranchised think because the life of the disenfranchised under apartheid made thinking apartheid, more than anything else, an absolute necessity. To think so as to know how to live the extant condition that was apartheid. To think so as to know how to *be* under apartheid *and* how to think for a life where apartheid no longer obtained.

To think apartheid, to think under apartheid, must be done, always and a priori, under the condition of perversity. I think apartheid knowing that, as Jacques Derrida says, "I cannot challenge it except by testifying to its omnipresence in me."[1] The very writing of *The Perversity of Gratitude: An Apartheid Education* is a testament to apartheid. *The Perversity of Gratitude* itself is an acknowledgment that, much as I spent a lifetime resisting apartheid, and much as I am still inclined, viscerally, to struggle against it, "It is me." I am constituted out of apartheid much as Derrida, positing himself, close to the end of his life, as an anticolonial Algerian in *Monolingualism*, is at pains to understand his fraught relationship to the French language.[2] Much as the French language is Jacques Derrida and Jacques Derrida is the French language, I, Grant Farred, always the symptomatic unrepresentable proper noun, am apartheid. (I am only a name among names. I am the name who writes all other names, even—or especially—those that remain unnamed but hauntologically, insistently present, breaking through the silence that is their not being named.) In my very speaking against apartheid, I speak it. I speak—and speak against—the enduring effect that is the perversity of my gratitude to apartheid.

Apartheid, both in a chronological sense (my generation was born after it was already a fact of political life)[3] and in an ideological sense, did not only precede me. Apartheid indisputably persists in me. *The Perversity of Gratitude*, however, must not be understood as the triumph of the logic that all resistance is futile. The perversity of my gratitude, rather, must be taken as the simultaneous writing of and against the "impassable." But as such, it is a writing mindful of, and perhaps even a little afraid of, the effects that such an undertaking will surely reveal. To write the perversity of gratitude is to write the self's thinking as unavoidably formed by—so that it is already indelibly marked by—the condition it is opposing. This is a perverse kind of autopoiesis, where the organization of complexity is at once reinforced by creativity as much as it is determined to undermine itself by insisting on the centrality of expressing gratitude where none is historically expected.

As such, it is a violent writing, this perverse autopoiesis, demanding to be done, aggressively nonnegotiable. It is a thinking that must be taken up, no matter the risks that might arise from this autopoiesis, the risks to the historically anti-apartheid self and to the disenfranchised self's sense of itself—a disenfranchised sense of self now made unimaginably precarious, always potentially subject to undoing itself. It is, however, not so much a matter of succumbing to the logic that resistance to the apartheid that "is me" is futile. *The Perversity of Gratitude* stands, rather, as the staging of the conflict, the conducting of a battle that feels awfully like the waging of a war (with and against the self) between my disenfranchised apartheid education and how it has manifested itself in me so that I must always reflect and acknowledge what it has made me— and, more disconcertingly, how it is in me, how I am indisputably of it, how constitutive it is of any writing that strives for the autopoietic, and how, I try to remind myself, it is of me, much as it never understood that then (maybe even now). It could never bring itself to acknowledge how constitutive of it I was, how formative disenfranchised thinking was to the apartheid regime's machinations, how the thinking subject of a disenfranchised education haunted the apartheid state in its waking hours, how much the thinking subject of a disenfranchised education was the stuff of their white supremacist nightmares. The only way to write autopoietically of a disenfranchised education is to do so through that concept that acknowledges, in its very self-naming, the intense complexities that constitute it and reside within it—those contradictions that barely hold together, that threaten, at any moment, to tear it apart; such is the autopoiesis of the perversity of gratitude.

Because of how indisputably I was of it, I am now able to assert that for the disenfranchised to live under apartheid, it was necessary to think. It was only possible, to render the matter hyperbolically (and yet not), to live apartheid by thinking apartheid.

And so, I testify:

Apartheid made me think. And for that I am grateful.

That is the perverse truth of my disenfranchised apartheid education.[4]

Structure: A Brief Word

As is titularly obvious, perversity and gratitude are the chief concepts that preoccupy me in this book. Thinking my apartheid education in relation to these concepts, however, is by no means a straightforward affair. It turns out that these primary concepts—thinking, perversity, and gratitude, and trying to understand how such a gratitude creates a debt to apartheid (itself the intensification of perversity)—and the many other concepts central to *The Perversity of Gratitude* are difficult, polyvalent, palimpsestic, sometimes maybe apprehended as a concatenation of insistent fragments,[5] constantly in autopoietic tension, multifarious in their construction, and require more than a single mode of critique to reveal themselves fully (or, at least, to reveal themselves more fully). It is, of course, impossible to exhaust any concept.[6]

To this end, *The Perversity of Gratitude* is organized around four chapters, each of which features one of my teachers. These figures appear chronologically, as I encountered them pedagogically: Richard Owen Dudley and Morgan MacArthur, who taught me at Livingstone High School; Stanley Gordon Moysey Ridge, my college professor at the University of the Western Cape (UWC) (Stan would have been, in South African parlance, my "university" professor); and Richard Moore Rive, who never taught me formally but from whom I learned a great deal as a consequence of a friendship that began during my graduate year at UWC. Interspersed among the chapters are definitions of the various concepts. The concepts do not appear in order of importance. However, as the grounding concepts, perversity, gratitude, and thinking come first. The definitions of the concepts are not meant to be the final word, nor can they be said to be, strictly speaking, provisional, because that would suggest a certain insecurity is attached to the concept. That is not the case. The definitions are, rather, a first thinking that is confident in its claims but only on the condition that it subjects itself always to a next thinking. These definitions constitute a first thinking that is subjected to further critique in the chapters. Concepts are thought again, revised, and maybe even reconceived in their second or seventh writing. The chapters show the concepts as always redolent with possibility.

The concepts are therefore a point of departure. Read chronologically, the structure of *The Perversity of Gratitude* could, as such, present a problem. Readers are likely to encounter a concept in a chapter before they have encountered its definition and are thus encouraged to skip forward or backward (to revisit the first articulation). Indeed, this may be the most advisable way to take up *The Perversity of Gratitude*—as a series of definitions that sometimes do not follow chronologically.

The concepts also work collaboratively, so that out of them, in their singularity and collectivity, an alternative anti-apartheid philosophical vocabulary offers itself. We derive, for example, entirely new possible understandings for gratitude in terms of how it works in relation to perversity. Complicating matters even more is the post–ipso facto nature of at least the titular conceptual delineations. After all, we can say that we are already in possession of at least a working definition of the titular concepts. That is indeed the case. However, as just noted, these concepts are already plenipotentiary—dependent upon another concept, a different concept with which it is already in relation.

In addition to the interspersed definitions, concepts are subjected to a further thinking in the interludes, which operate in their own distinct register. More philosophical in tone, the interludes stand as yet one more attempt to "unconceal"—Martin Heidegger's term—that which is constitutive of the concepts or has not yet been thought in relation to the concepts.

The principle at work here is Deleuzian. Out of repetition, Gilles Deleuze argues, emerges difference,[7] and out of difference, the possibility of the unthought. And the true measure of a thinker's work, says Heidegger,[8] is the fecundity of his unthought.

Because repetition is so constitutive a feature of *The Perversity of Gratitude*, it enjoys a sui generis location. Repetition is defined not as a concept along with the other concepts; rather, it is tucked into the interlude that follows the second chapter, explicated as a feature of disenfranchised education. To say, then, that perversity and gratitude are the titular concepts is to say nothing. Every concept, from thinking to the dialectic to the diaspora-in-place, comes into its own prominence, and, true to themselves, each one of these concepts emerges according to its own schedule, punctual only to itself. Some concepts manifest their importance in predictable moments, while others arise almost unexpectedly, appearing as if out of nowhere—and yet not. These concepts lie quietly in wait, ready to burst into life at precisely that moment when the thinking demands its articulation. Autoimmunity provides us with another such instance, preceding repetition in the same interlude and then rising up to address what the moment needs. Autoimmunity announces itself in a fashion at once untimely and yet punctual. The concept, in *The Perversity of Gratitude*, knows its moment, and it will seize that moment without hesitation, full of confidence in its timing.

By any account, *The Perversity of Gratitude* is organized unconventionally. It may be, however, that it is a work cut according to its cloth, as a discussion of such concepts necessitates an unconventional structure. The singularity of the structure presents itself in the next section, which belongs to none of the aforementioned categories. The section that immediately follows this one is neither chapter nor interlude. It bears some resemblance to the definition of concepts, but it is not that either. It seeks simply to prepare the ground for what is to come—chapter, definition, interlude—and so contains within it elements of each.

Acknowledgments

It was a struggle to write *The Perversity of Gratitude*. It was a project whose form was long in coming. It is a project with which I have lived for many years, perhaps even dating back to that first moment in January 1976, when I entered Livingstone High School. I cannot mark its beginning with any certainty—nor, in truth, do I wish to.

That I was able to find a form that could fit what needed to be said and how to say it is due almost entirely to my remarkable editor, Ryan Mulligan. Even in those moments when I turned away from the project, he reminded me that it needed to be written. Ryan read this work with a careful, patient eye, helping me to hone it into shape, encouraging me at critical junctures, and always pushing in such a way that I came to see what was needed. Once more, Mr. Mulligan, you have my heartfelt thanks.

I am grateful to my friends Vashna Jagernath and Richard Pithouse for inviting me to present one of the earliest articulations of this project to an audience of trade unionists in Johannesburg in 2017. I recall with fondness the unexpectedly positive response from the audience. Similar thanks are due to Dana Nelson for inviting me to Vanderbilt University in the fall of 2017.

I would also like to thank one of my readers, Sharad Chari, for his insistence that I be more critical of Martin Heidegger. I have no doubt that I have fallen short in this regard, but I promise, Sharad, I really did try to subject Heidegger to as intense a scrutiny as I could in the rewriting.

Shaun Viljoen, my friend of more than forty years, read the manuscript and offered both support and the ready grammatical red pen of the old English teacher that he was—and, I am sure, that he remains, even in semiretirement. We've come a long way from that moment in 1979 when we climbed the Cedarberg Mountains. Shaun, I wrote the Richard chapter with you very much in my mind.

To those classmates who have remained, in the many decades after we no longer darkened the hallways of 100 Lansdowne Road, an important part of my life: My debt is substantial. Your friendship has meant more to me than I could ever have imagined when our paths first crossed.

To Penny (1972): You are an artist possessed of more talents than any one person should be able to command. Yours is that spirit that brings life and laughter to all who have known you. I miss not seeing you, Penny.

To Des (1976): You remain, to this day, as you have always been and will always be, unimpugnable. I write this with love.

To Merlyn (1978): Your salient characteristic has always been to call things as you see it. The best thing about that characteristic is how it is inflected with acuity, generosity, loyalty, and warmth. It is a matter of import to me that we are in regular touch.

To Thommo (1977): How you maintain your ecumenical disposition is beyond me, but what a fine job you do of it. Thommo, I remember the flair of your cover drive. I shrink from your indefatigability; whenever I'm in Cape Town, Thommo, you find me, and this irks me because I'd rather remain undetected.

To B. (1977): This is above all to B., for mountains climbed, for mischief engaged in (stones on a tin roof), for the clubs we hit, for the music we listened to, for those conversations we had and continue to have—conversations that have, over the last thirty-four years, been conducted across the Atlantic. Mainly, Broer, this is for forty-five years of friendship.

You were so much more than a spectral presence to me as I wrote this book.

My teachers were intellectuals; I have been fortunate.

R. O. Dudley possessed a brilliant mind. That he disbursed that brilliance to a sometimes-wayward high school student like me strikes me, especially now that he is gone and I am left to consider his brilliance, as an act of immense intellectual magnanimity. Like many others who passed through Livingstone High School, I will be forever touched by the richness, the variegation, the easy intensity, and, most importantly, the sheer presence of his thinking. That out of South Africa—and by this I mean the state in toto, not just from out of the ranks of the disenfranchised—emerged such a mind continues to be a thing of wonder to me.

"Mrs. MacArthur" was, and continues to be, more than a teacher to me. She has the great gift of being able to see what is possible before anyone else. She has a prescient sense of how the world might unfold, and she, in almost my earliest encounter with her, opened prospects for me that lay beyond my visage and were not even a speck on the horizon that was my imaginary. She is the best English teacher I could ever have hoped to have. I am privileged to have been her student.

Stan Ridge was a man of the institution, in the best possible sense. He believed fervently in the work of making UWC the most serious intellectual place it could be, beginning with its Department of English and extending to the various high administrative offices he held. My intellectual training began at Livingstone, but I truly took to learning with gusto and joy under Stan and the English Department's tutelage at UWC. Stan gave UWC everything he had, and then some. I owe my passage to graduate school in the United States to Stan. I owe him and his wife Elaine Ridge so much more. At some indefinable point, he became my friend. In moments of quiet reflection, he is with me still.

Richard Rive embraced the role he had crafted for himself: To be larger than life, to hold forth with supreme confidence, to affect an above-it-allness that verged on pomposity. Soon after Tiananmen Square Day, however, I came to understand more fully how manufactured that role was, for all its flawless execution. What a price you paid for the performance you delivered. I cannot think about Richard without an admixture of sadness and gratitude. He prepared me for academic life in a way that no one else could have. He was generous with his time, he was kind, and he had about him a unique joie de vivre. You deserved a different world, Richard, one that would have allowed you to be yourself. The circumstances of your death and the injustice that followed haunt me still.

Grant Farred: LHS (1976), UWC (1981), Ithaca (2022)

The Perversity of Gratitude

Gratitude

In Three Steps

Step I: I Feel Gratitude toward My Experience of Oppression

Surely only those with a perverse cast of mind could possibly express gratitude for their experience of oppression. The possibility of expressing gratitude, as a subject disenfranchised by apartheid in South Africa, for having been oppressed should not bear thinking. No less perverse is giving thanks for having, as a student oppressed by apartheid, received what was condemned, quite correctly, as an "inferior education." Oppression and structural educational inequality, located within the turbulent history of disenfranchised resistance to the apartheid state, spanning roughly two decades, from 1972 to 1989, are the objective political truths against which *The Perversity of Gratitude* has chosen to do battle.

The titular concepts of perversity and gratitude ground this project and will thus occupy us extensively here. Gratitude and perversity are thought together in this project—a project that blends political and philosophical critique with personal reflection, that melds tributes to four pedagogical figures with a recapitulation of two educational institutions, and that both affords definitions to and redefines concepts in the course of the larger writing. Because these concepts are interlocking, they are impossible to disentangle. Gratitude and perversity inflect, shape, distort, and give final form to each other in their being considered together. Undertaken here is the making perverse of gratitude and the uncovering of gratitude in an experience most perverse.

The Perversity of Gratitude expresses gratitude for having been educated, as a disenfranchised subject, under the system of apartheid. It conveys gratitude for having been afforded what anti-apartheid activists (including me and many in my generation) denounced, as they should have, as a "second-class" or "gutter" education at the height of the anti-apartheid struggle, in the period from 1976 to the late 1980s.

Such an expression of gratitude could easily stand as the very definition of the perversity of gratitude—a gratitude that, by all accounts, should be unsustainable. And yet, decades later, this gratitude for apartheid education continues to present itself as a pedagogical truth that will not be stilled. It will not be refused. It demands, against any and all conventional expectation, to be voiced. It insists on making itself known.

To pronounce such a perverse gratitude is to fly in the face of an axiomatic logic that declares that there should indeed be no gratitude expressed for those institutions, practices, and, perhaps most of all, people who engaged in the business of oppressing on the basis of race—of disenfranchising, disempowering, impoverishing, and discriminating against others because they were not white—and who, by occupying their lofty position (as bureaucrats, state functionaries, teachers, members of police and security forces, and so on), benefited from their capacity and power to oppress. This contradiction in terms is only intensified when the perverse gratitude acknowledges the formative pedagogical role played by white South African teachers, in the aforementioned two institutions, in the education of the historically disenfranchised and when those historically enfranchised teachers are thanked for having taught gutter education to disenfranchised students named "coloured" (mixed-race), "Indian," and "black" by the apartheid authorities.

Perverse, is it not? Gratitude would seem unimaginable in such circumstances.

What kind of education for the disenfranchised could apartheid have provided other than one damaging or detrimental to the disenfranchised mind?

And yet, I am determined in my position, no matter the apparent perversity. I am grateful that I received the education I did at Livingstone High School, in Cape Town's leafy southern suburbs, where the entire student body—but not the teachers, critically, as we will see—was composed of coloured students from the Western Cape. I am grateful that I was educated, at the tertiary level, at UWC, an institution of higher learning founded in 1960 by the apartheid regime and reserved exclusively for coloureds. UWC was conceived so as to deny coloureds access to South Africa's premier university, the University of Cape Town (UCT). Almost all white, UCT was established in 1829, a full 130 years before UWC. (UCT is today, and has been for some time, Africa's most prestigious university.)

I am unshakable in my gratitude, no matter the nefarious pedagogical designs of the apartheid regime. Out of the milieu that was Livingstone and other coloured high schools like it, a poetic phrase had emerged, decades before my generation darkened its halls, to describe ideologically what coloured education was designed to achieve: "Education for Barbarism." Education for coloureds was administered by the Coloured Affairs Department (CAD), which had its racist equivalents in the Bantu Education Department (BAD)[1] for blacks and the Indian Education Department (IAD) for disenfranchised South Africans who traced their lineage—regardless of how far back that lineage ran—to the Asian subcontinent (that is, contemporary India, Pakistan, and Bangladesh).

"Education for Barbarism," a slogan which I attend to later, was coined by I. B. Tabata, a leading figure in anti-apartheid pedagogical circles. Tabata's is a resonant phrase, stinging in its rebuke to apartheid's master planners. It is also catchy as an oppositional rallying cry.

It is a phrase to which my generation, who entered Livingstone in 1976, the year of the famed Soweto student rebellion, gravitated and is one we invoked frequently.

Regardless of Tabata's indictment of CAD education, the perversity of my gratitude seems only to intensify.

How could I, a member of the 1976 generation who protested so fierce-
ly against our CAD gutter education, who found historical force, biblical in its denunciation of apartheid education, in Tabata's phrase, insist
upon gratitude to my apartheid education?

Step II: I Must Be Forgetting the Right Thing and Remembering the Wrong Thing

Anamnesis is the forgetting of things from a supposedly previous experience. A question is thereby raised: What does ascription to the perversity
of gratitude forget and what does it remember? Anamnesis is a danger,
then, because it makes possible the forgetting of that which is ostensibly
right, disenfranchised apartheid education as a "barbaric" force. Con-
versely, and by implication, anamnesis can be said—and said only in the
spirit of perversity, which is to say, without any great confidence—to be
that process that engenders remembering the wrong thing. Worse still is
not only that anamnesis causes us to remember the wrong thing; in a
perverse rendering of anamnesis, such as the one offered here, we are encouraged to remember the wrong thing affirmatively as that thing that
must be taken into our care and that we must retrieve lest it, as Martin
Heidegger understands it, withdraw. In its withdrawing from us, we not
only lose this thing—lose sight of it, forget it, forget to remember its essence—we leave it unthought. Anamnesis is how we guard against the
withdrawal of that which must be thought, that which must not be lost
from memory and must not be lost because of the repressive force that
history can sometimes be.

However, the effect of conceiving anamnesis perversely is that it
facilitates the recovery of things from a previous experience that any
orthodox account would prefer to remain forgotten or unthought.
Through the perversity of gratitude, anamnesis becomes the process by
which that which is supposed to be forgotten continues to resonate; that
which was supposed to be forgotten demands, in the face of considerable
opposition, a second or post–ipso facto life. That which was supposed
to be forgotten comes to life rupturously,[2] insisting that it be thought,
and in so doing, it threatens the hegemonic power of history over the

present. Anamnesis, thought in its relation to the perversity of gratitude, irrupts out of and against the logic of the present; what Michel Foucault would render as the "ontology of the present."[3] Through anamnesis, the perversity of gratitude, which must be taken here as the haunting of the present by a past (apartheid) that was long since presumed to have been made irredeemable by the political dispensation of the present (the non-racist postapartheid state), draws the present in its entirety into question. The hauntology of/from the past, figured here as the perversity of gratitude, casts a long, interrogative shadow on the present, piercing the political armor granted to the present by the unspeakable facticity of the past—the often brutal, state-orchestrated transgression against the disenfranchised that was apartheid. The perversity of gratitude presents a particular challenge to the present because it is conceived as a position of absolute, unrelenting opposition. As such, anamnesis intensifies the conceptual force of the perversity of gratitude, adding a sharper edge to the titular concept in both its singularity and as a composite.

Through the perversity of gratitude, anamnesis inverts the order of things as they are expected to be. Instead of forgetting the wrong thing and remembering the right thing, the perversity of gratitude works perversely. While it does not exactly make us forget the right thing—apartheid as a racist oppression—it insists on remembering the wrong thing. More than that, the perversity of gratitude does not only make us remember the wrong thing; it also assigns signal importance to what might in conventional (anti-apartheid) historical terms be, a priori, condemned. The dominant anti-apartheid logic, with good reason, determines that disenfranchised apartheid education was bad (institutional pun unavoidable) for the minds of the disenfranchised. As such, the perversity of gratitude confounds conventional anti-apartheid logic. It does so, however, not to rationalize the deleterious effects of apartheid education or to excuse the inexcusable intellectual violence that apartheid committed against the disenfranchised.

Au contraire. As the governing concept in this writing, the perversity of gratitude reveals the unthought and the entirely unexpected effects of a disenfranchised apartheid education.

My disenfranchised apartheid education had an unexpected outcome.

My apartheid education made me think.

And thinking about thinking, thinking about what thinking is, as engaged here through Heidegger's work in a series of postwar lectures called *Was Heißt Denken?* (*What Is Called Thinking?*), is the core preoccupation of *The Perversity of Gratitude*.

In the classroom where the disenfranchised took their lessons, they learned to meditate on thinking. They were given the opportunity to think about thinking. It was in those classrooms, more than anywhere else, that the disenfranchised were trained to think about thinking.

Conceptually, it is only through the perverse insistence on expressing gratitude for what is widely deemed to be the wrong thing that the unanticipated value of what the apartheid regime intended to be an inferior education can be uncovered. Brought, through perverse means, out of its overdetermined apartheid context, it is shown to have been a fertile breeding ground for thinking—precisely the opposite of what the apartheid regime, with its BADs and CADs, intended. This shows CAD education in a completely new and philosophically revealing—dare one say flattering?—light. It shows CAD education as philosophical, even by Heidegger's exacting standards, because, as we know, for Heidegger, "only philosophy thinks"[4] It is possible for the disenfranchised to learn thinking to think and to learn to think philosophically, even under the most oppressive material conditions. *The Perversity of Gratitude* makes Heidegger's commitment to thinking unrecognizable to him in that disenfranchised apartheid education is now presented and understood less as an impediment or a structural pedagogical obstacle to thinking and more as a philosophical provocation—a philosophical proving ground, we might even suggest.

BAD, CAD, and IAD education was born out of a racist policy, making it a racist, nefarious, and anti-intellectual pedagogical undertaking. After all, the work of the intellectual is to think, and CAD was designed to quash any pedagogical propensity, inclination, or opportunity to train the disenfranchised to think. CAD education did not even imagine that out of its proscribed syllabi for the disenfranchised, Heidegger's question—"What is thinking?"—could arise.

But arise it did, even if it did not assume a form in any way familiar to Heidegger. Livingstone High School was certainly not an institution that Heidegger would have conceived of as a philosophical training ground.

And Heidegger's question arose only because the perversity of gratitude gives precedence to remembering the wrong thing. It would, after all, be difficult, and tantamount to political suicide and intellectual negligence, to forget the right thing.

In postapartheid South Africa, because of a range of factors, the predations of the black ruling elite (corruption, nepotism, state capture—that class against whom Frantz Fanon inveighed so strongly in *The Wretched of the Earth*)[5] and the long afterlife of white minority rule primary among them, the lingering aftereffects of apartheid's inequalities remain all too palpable.

Visible in almost every sphere of public life and in the national education system at least as much, if not more, than anywhere else, inequality is the order of the day. The black ruling elite has secured for its children access to those institutions of learning reserved, under apartheid, for whites. For children of the historically disenfranchised, by far the majority, the situation in education has changed—and *not* for the better.

I venture to say this without fear of contradiction: The 1976 generation of disenfranchised students and those who preceded us (dating back to, say, the late 1940s—that is, the parents of the 1976 generation), as well as those who, until around 1990, succeeded us, were afforded a *better* education than students from a similar class background have access to in contemporary South Africa. That is, lower-middle-class and working-class disenfranchised students received a better education than their peers today. I say this with authority because I, like others who attended Livingstone or other such CAD high schools, emerged out of the ranks of the disenfranchised (Cape Flats) working class.

The apartheid regime did not know—could not have known—what possibilities for thinking, what intellectual kernels, were contained within the education it prescribed, and sought to vigilantly oversee, for the disenfranchised.

The perversity of gratitude is truly perverse. It is truly perverse because one of this form of gratitude's founding premises is the recognition that the will to know thinking must dismiss, almost out of hand, the right thing. Perversely, it turns out, the right thing—decrying the intellectual violence intended by apartheid education for the disenfranchised—provides poor soil for the work of thinking thinking; *das Denken denken* would be its correct accusative grammatical rendering.[6] In Heidegger's terms, the right thing does not know that it is not thinking. The right thing, to its great intellectual cost, does not take up the question of thinking. Wrongly, the right thing does not even, in any philosophical way, take up the question of thinking, to say nothing of thinking for what thinking is. The right thing does not draw what it incorrectly presumes it already knows (again, thinking is not presented as a question by the right thing) into question. The right thing at no point makes of thinking a question. Thinking is certainly not a question on which the right thing trains its philosophical sights. It does not make of thinking a question.

"We do not know what thinking is."[7]

And it is precisely because we do not know that we must think (for) thinking.

Step III: Forgetting and Remembering

The perversity of gratitude stipulates that it is imperative to forget the right thing and remember the wrong thing. As such, anamnesis and the perversity of gratitude do not stand in contrast. Anamnesis and the perversity of gratitude operate, rather, in a necessarily difficult conjunction. These concepts amplify and complicate each other; they lend each other philosophical depth and a rare explicatory force in their being thought together. They function, in the most provocative sense, in "non-accordance"—to use a Heideggerian concept. (The dialectic is by far the dominant concept used to explicate the tensions between forces in *The Perversity of Gratitude*. In the course of this writing, I attend to the dialectic. However, in accounting for the relationship between forgetting and remembering, *non-accordance* is preferred.)

To be in non-accordance is to recognize a relation that functions not primarily through the logic of opposites. (Such a path ensures that we will arrive at the dialectic.) Non-accordance, rather, highlights the perverse (or surprising) inversion of the order of things—remembering the wrong thing, forgetting the right thing—out of which is produced a novel form of intellectual tension. Out of non-accordance emerges a dissonance—and a strange resonance—between forgetting and remembering that works to shed a mutually illuminating light, one on the other.

To be in non-accordance is to be, in Shakespeare's terms, "out of joint"[8] with the prevailing tenor of the anti- and postapartheid time as well as with the dominant understanding of anti-apartheid history.

The effect of the perversity of gratitude on anamnesis is that their being thought together mitigates all forms of absolute forgetting and demands of us that we remember the very (wrong) thing we would rather forget. The perversity of gratitude bears testament to the persistence, in one way or another, of that which the dominant account of history would rather have us forget. For the sake of advancing the argument, let us offer anamnesis as not only the impossibility of forgetting (that is, the persistence of memory—that which is resolute in its determination to return, that specter of what was that threatens to, in moments when we least expect it, haunt us) but the impropriety of memory. Forgetting the right thing is merely the prelude to the rude return that is remembering the wrong thing. Anamnesis awakens the disenfranchised, anti-apartheid self to the historic persistence of the wrong thing. The perversity of gratitude is, in short, the most rigorous thinking that could only emerge out of a disenfranchised thinking of a gutter apartheid education—a gutter education, it turns out, that was nothing if not conducive to training the disenfranchised to think. To think a disenfranchised apartheid education, it is necessary, then, to recognize or to simply extract what was not so dormant all along (the inclining toward thinking)—the intellectual worth of that which the dominant understanding of a BAD or CAD education worked determinedly to make its disenfranchised charges forget: In every pedagogical encounter, there is the possibility for thinking, for thinking to take place, for thinking to be taught. Such a possibility exists in every pedagogical encounter, no matter how racist the regime in power, no matter how lacking the material resources might be, no matter how oppressive the conditions of everyday life.

The perversity of gratitude is nothing less than the impropriety of giving thanks to that which it would appear no thanks should properly be given. Thanks, perhaps more than anything, should be withheld, with good historical reason, if we remember the violence that apartheid sought to do to the disenfranchised mind. *The Perversity of Gratitude*, as an account of giving thanks, directly contradicts the argument, one sanctioned by history, that a disenfranchised expression of gratitude for an apartheid education is simply historically wrong.[9] It is perverse to give thanks (*Danke* in Heidegger's German, *Dankie* in Afrikaans) for that which is entirely undeserving of thanks (disenfranchised apartheid education) and for that which we have every reason (certainly every good political reason) to regard with approbation—or worse, that which we should, whether it goes by the name of BAD, CAD, or IAD, without so much as a second thought, condemn.

The Perversity of Gratitude remembers the wrong thing at the cost of forgetting the right thing at the very moment that second thoughts become the condition for thinking disenfranchised apartheid education against the grain of received historical (anti- and postapartheid) wisdom—that is the moment when the perversity of gratitude announces itself, when it marks the improper as a rupturous historical statement. The impropriety that is remembering the wrong thing is a perverse expression of gratitude that opens up and reveals a fertile ground for thinking, a ground where apartheid education had intended that no thinking take place.

Gratitude, then, is the gift of a debt that had no intention of being created. Gratitude is the perversity of the gift made by thinking out of that historical context where no thinking was supposed to be possible. In unintentionally making this gift, the effect of the gift made by apartheid education is to create, against all historical expectation, a debt where none was intended. CAD education is the gift made by the apartheid regimes that, philosophically, at least, keeps on giving. The perversity of the gift of a gutter education is that it is a gift that possessed no awareness of its value as a philosophical gift.

Concepts 1

These brief outlines of each concept are, as we already know, by no means exhaustive. The conceptual delineations serve only to give us a first articulation, one that even then can arguably be described as provisional. The grounding premise is, as it must be, that every articulation is a priori and constitutively insufficient. The brief conceptual delineations are a provisional point of reference—a first, but by no means the only or the last, place from which to begin a thinking of the concept. As offered here, the concept invites and opens up to the possibilities that flow from its individual and its contextual—in relation to one or more other concepts—thinking.

Furthermore, the concepts are not delineated in the same way. Some are more conceptually thought than others, and some are rendered etymologically, enabling—demanding, almost—a more expansive thinking or calling for a more rigorous critique. For this reason, they are offered in the ways that seem most useful for an initial engagement. They are offered in what is, for the purposes of *The Perversity of Gratitude*, the order of their conceptual importance. However, these concepts complicate and irradiate each other, and the order they appear in is itself a matter that can be argued. Structurally, it might have been better to disseminate the definitions before each concept was discussed. There is certainly merit to such an arrangement. However, with such an organization, there is the risk of disruption and inconsistency. The gathering and ordering of the concepts allows, at the very least, for easy reference.

Some concepts, as might already be obvious, run throughout *The Perversity of Gratitude*; others appear less frequently. There is every reason to draw the order of the concepts into question. The "inaccuracy" of the order of the concepts may have everything to do with how the concepts are enmeshed in one another. Sometimes the concepts are so caught up in each other that they form a blended singularity. In other moments, one concept will put another into the shade, seemingly delaying the other its right to come into its own. Such is the fate that the concept has to endure when it is made to live its life as a plenipotentiary, a foreigner representing itself in a foreign conceptual land.

We begin with, then, not the governing concepts but thinking. When we do attend to the concepts, it will be first in their singularity and then, in three iterations, in how it is they work together.

Thinking/*Denke*

Perversity and gratitude, for all their titular centrality, remain secondary concepts—that is, they are concepts that turn on what it means to think. Their definitions will follow. Before all else, we must attend to thinking—thinking as thought by Heidegger. Of all the philosophers of the twentieth century, it is Heidegger alone who insists on thinking as the fundamental question of our Being in the world. In order to be in the world, we must *think* our *Being* (*Sein*). Heidegger thinks about thinking in order that we might know (how to think) Being. "We do not know what thinking is," Heidegger declares, "but we do know when we are not thinking."[1]

Ostensibly, Heidegger begins in negation: "We do *not* know." But the negation exists only on the surface. Heidegger's negation is, in truth, an affirmation. We know when we do not know. We therefore know when we are thinking. At the very least, we can "intuit," a concept of some importance to Heidegger, when we are thinking.[2] (We have some sense, some grasp, no matter how faint, of when it is we are undertaking the work of thinking. This does not mean, however, that we can ever be sure that we *are* thinking. Thinking about whether we are in fact thinking can thus be said to be the first order of the work of thinking, even as we can never be sure that we *know* what thinking is.)[3] Again, on the surface, Heidegger presents the problem of not thinking as a matter of temporality. We know when we are not thinking. The prospect that Heidegger opens in and through his negation is potentiality; we can know when we are thinking. Heidegger's negation is thus better understood as an acknowledgment girded by an injunction. Heidegger's negation is above all a call to interrogative arms—to know what it means to think, beginning from the premise that we do not know (do not yet know, under optimal conditions) what thinking is.

It is to the injunction, the making imperative of thinking, that we must attend. To know what it means to think demands that human beings must learn how to attune themselves temporally. Human beings must demand of themselves that they attend to those many moments (by far the majority of our waking lives) when they are, as is human habit, not thinking. If we think about thinking, then it becomes possible to not only guard against not thinking but also to identify those moments when we are thinking.

This is the germ of possibility that Heidegger offers—that we can know thinking when we know the moment in which we *are* thinking.

To know thinking, to know what thinking is, is to be in possession of a definition of thinking. To know thinking is not, then, only a matter of temporal recognition—of knowing what the moment holds within itself. It is the definition of *thinking*, of knowing what it is we are doing when we think, of understanding how it is we come to think, that eludes Heidegger, that lies frustratingly beyond his philosophical grasp. That is the philosophical difficulty with which Heidegger grapples in *Was Heißt Denken?*

Heidegger's call to thinking, if these are the conditions of his struggle, is sometimes apprehended less as an injunction than an invitation. (The distinction between the two, however, is hardly clearly delineated.) The philosopher is extending his hand for us to join him as he locates himself in the company of, inter alia, the ancients (perhaps Socrates, above all), Friedrich Nietzsche (*Thus Spoke Zarathustra's* "last man" is of particular interest to Heidegger), and poet Friedrich Hölderlin in producing a definition—a philosophical delineation—that can clarify for us what it means to think.

In advance, we know that we are not capable of such a task. However, our philosophical—or conceptual, as Gilles Deleuze might prefer—inability is hardly what matters. (Deleuze, we remember, understands philosophy as the production of concepts. So understood, our work here is to produce *thinking* as a concept that emerges out of our need to explicate as fully as possible why our governing concept, the perversity of gratitude, depends so much on thinking.) At stake, rather, is a historico-philosophical recognition that is also a philosophical commitment—*das Denken denken*, meaning that we think, in every possible moment, about thinking. This involves thinking about what it means to think, regardless of whether everything is at risk or nothing is on the line, and guarding, through our thinking about thinking, against not thinking. Of course, if everything is at stake, it matters greatly that we think in that moment.

It is only when we think about thinking that we can begin to approach what it means to be in the world. To render the matter as a proto-Heideggerian formula, *Sein = das Denken denken*.

Thinking about thinking is the intellectual undertaking that defines *The Perversity of Gratitude*. This writing does not even approach a definition of thinking. What it does seek to do, however, is to think about thinking in a range of registers. Thinking is what grounds this writing. *The Perversity of Gratitude* is, in this way, a taking up of Heidegger's struggle under conditions—racial oppression girded by a virulent white supremacy—that presented itself to him in the form of National Socialism but about which he never, in any substantive, sustained, Heideggerian way, thought.

Better still, we might say it is not so much that which is unthought in Heidegger as it is that which remains deliberately under-thought that compels us, because of what Heidegger does not think, to think National Socialism. How is it possible to leave unthought that mode of being in the world that so pertinently raises the *Dasein* of a people as the first order of being? (*Dasein*, for our purposes, can be taken to be mean "being there," "being in the world," "existence," mode of being in the world, always with the understanding that it is always inflected with the possibility of "thrownness" or "falling.")[4] Heidegger let be, and not in any Heideggerian sense of *letting be*, that which he should have subjected to thinking. In Heidegger's case, what remains unthought by the preeminent thinker of thinking is not so much the failure to think as it is the deliberate turning away from thinking. Here, the unthought of a thinker points as much to the richness of what resides in the unthought as to make suspect that of which he knew but would not think—even when it is precisely what he should, above all, have made fit for this thinking. As much as Heidegger failed history, he failed philosophy. Despite his lifelong investment in philosophy, it is in his failing philosophy that Heidegger is, by his own standards, found most wanting.

The paradox Heidegger provokes in regard to *The Perversity of Gratitude* is a sharp one. It is precisely because of Heidegger's unthought that disenfranchised apartheid education must not remain unthought. For the unthought to remain unthought is among the signal greatest affronts to thinking. How is it that Heidegger could have failed himself rather than think National Socialism?

He dissembled about National Socialism nowhere more so than in the *Der Spiegel* interview that was published posthumously in 1976, after having been conducted a decade earlier. The posthumous publication was per Heidegger's request. (A historical irony is that Heidegger died on May 26, 1976, exactly three weeks before the Soweto uprising on June 16, 1976.) His antisemitism comes through clearly, no matter what Heideggerian apologists would say, in *Schwartze Hefte* (*The Black Notebooks*).[5]

However, to think Heidegger's thinking, to think with and/or because of Heidegger, is always, as Jacques Derrida reminds us, a difficult undertaking that almost unfailingly draws us closer to Heidegger, regardless of whether or not we are determined to take our distance from him:

> From the moment one is having it out with [s'explique avec] with Heidegger in a critical or deconstructive fashion, must one not continue to recognize a certain necessity of his thinking, its character, which is inaugural in so many respects, and especially what remains to come for us in its deciphering? This is a task of thinking, a historical task and a political task. A discourse on Nazism that dispenses with this task remains the conformist opinion of "good conscience."[6]

The necessity of Heidegger's thinking begins and ends, as it must, with Heidegger's thinking thinking. It is Heidegger's thinking thinking that constitutes the inaugural character of his work. There is, then, no way to have it out with Heidegger that does not call for an extended engagement with his thinking—an engagement that is as fraught with danger as it is filled with prospect, a prospect that promises new philosophical findings, new insights, and a renewed commitment (once again) to thinking. In this regard, "what is to come for us in its deciphering" exceeds the confines, important as these tasks might be, of the historical and the political. Instead, what is to come for us in its deciphering depends less on Heidegger and more on who it is who finds promise in Heidegger's oeuvre and on what it is that those who Heidegger so easily disparaged and dismissed are able to think because of his work. The Perversity of Gratitude is what is brought forth when Heidegger's symptomatic "Senegalese," that figure of blackness whose capacity he summarily denies in Was Heißt Denken?, thinks Heidegger, is drawn to thinking, and is made, we might even say, to think because of Heidegger.

It is for this reason that we would, of course, as Derrida warns us, be wrong to suggest that this thinking that comes to us courtesy of our deciphering (of Heidegger) is possible sans Heidegger. Such a deciphering is impossible without his thinking. What is more, any serious engagement with Heidegger's thinking must, perforce, a priori, pronounce itself impatient and unsatisfied with any critique that cannot rise above the level of "good conscience." To invoke good conscience is to rationalize nonengagement with a thinker who is necessary, if we follow Derrida, to every thinker who seeks to do the work of thinking. As such, the thinker Heidegger comes to us as necessary and as a figure of immense philosophical, historical, and political difficulty. We do not think with Heidegger, no matter that we do so in good conscience, at our peril, and at the cost of thinking thinking. It is no wonder, then, that Derrida names his contemplation "Heidegger, the Philosopher's Hell." To engage Heidegger is to come face-to-face with a fundamental philosophical difficulty. It is to recognize the thinker as a philosophical touchstone whose very thinking is marred, marked, overdetermined, and made objectionable by the thinker's actions or his failure to act, by what he says as well as by what he did not say, by those whom he holds in esteem and those whom he deems unworthy of consideration; the list is long. In thinking Heidegger, we are always aware of our proximity to what is politically untenable and historically violent; and, because of our proximity, we are left to ponder what it is that is unthought in our thinking.

However, even as we present ourselves with the difficulty that is our being drawn to and dependent on Heidegger's thinking, we affirm, regardless of our intentions, Heidegger's founding tenet. He is our guide—and by no means an infallible one—to thinking thinking. All our questions derive from him. We are, whether we acknowledge it or not, in debt to his thinking thinking. Any succumbing to the pitfalls of good conscience would constitute nothing so much as the failure to think thinking. And no amount of good conscience, as Derrida makes clear, can compensate for the work of thinking.

On the face of it, then, Heidegger's centrality to *The Perversity of Gratitude*'s thinking could not be, at once, more ironic or more appropriate. The irony, of course, is historically obvious. The philosophical touchstone for a critique of the racism that was disenfranchised apartheid education is a German philosopher who was, if one is being polite (and Derrida is not—he names it a "discourse on

Nazism"), a National Socialist fellow traveler. For Heidegger, that figure named a black thinker is entirely inconceivable, as I have written elsewhere.[7] However, it is precisely because of those conditions—racism, racial discrimination, disenfranchising particular constituencies within the *Lebensraum*—that Heidegger will not think that *das Denken denken* stands at the very heart of *The Perversity of Gratitude*. *Das Denken denken* is the founding provocation: Thinking for thinking; thinking thinking, beyond and despite the imaginary of the *Lebensraum* (the expansive national territory that was supposed to constitute the German state under National Socialism); and thinking thinking, particularly under those conditions where thinking is militated against institutionally, which is to say, as fundamental to a national political project. As has been made clear by now, the perversity, as well as the gratitude, of this writing is that it is more faithful to the Heideggerian injunction—*das Denken denken*, to think always for thinking—than Heidegger himself. This is true regardless of the location and despite the conditions (or, more accurately, precisely because of the conditions). The absolute democratization of thinking is the universalization of the call that is *das Denken denken*. It involves insisting, no matter Heidegger's explicit exclusion of the black mind, that all, without exception, must heed the call to think thinking.

To think the perversity of gratitude is to think Heidegger's unthought. Heidegger's unthought forms the fundament of what it is the perversity of gratitude is given to think and how it is the perversity of gratitude is given to think thinking.[8] The perversity of gratitude speaks to the extent to which "Heidegger's 'thinking' destabilizes the foundations of philosophy and the human sciences."[9] Are the foundations of philosophy and the human sciences so destabilized by Heidegger that hell is the only place from which it is possible to think? Can the philosopher's heaven then be said to be an arid, infertile location that is antithetical to thinking? Are all philosophers not better off in hell, the thinkers' nirvana?

At its core, then, no matter the protestations offered here, regardless of the difficulties addressed only insufficiently, irrespective of the ability to pronounce only provisionally what thinking is, *The Perversity of Gratitude* is a response to Heidegger's injunction; it is a response to his call to think before all else and to take joy in thinking above anything else. *The Perversity of Gratitude* is a writing against any and all moments in which *We do not know* might hold sway. Thinking thinking is "all" *The Perversity of Gratitude* endeavors to do—a Sisyphean exercise, surely, to say nothing of rendering thinking in so singular an anti-Heideggerian Heideggerian formulation already in struggle with anti- and postapartheid logic, to which must now be added this irresolvable conflict with Heidegger. This conflict acknowledges his thinking as fundament while eschewing his politics, as if these could ever be properly disarticulated. One perversity, a lifelong gratitude for a disenfranchised education, intensifies this other one, a debt to Heidegger's thinking that stretches back years. One gratitude is deepened and made more perverse by the other.

This perversity confounds.

This gratitude demands an apology, does it not?

This perversity offers thinking as that which emanates from it as an unimpugnable defense, and because of this solid defense, it refuses to apologize to history.

This gratitude is of such a magnitude that it stands as a gratitude for which no apology can be offered.

Gratitude

Gratitude is the gift of a debt that had no intention of being created. Gratitude is the perversity of the gift made by thinking out of that historical context where no thinking was intended. In unintentionally making this gift, the effect of the gift is to create, against all historical expectation, a debt where none was intended; this debt can only be described as perverse, so seemingly unworthy is the recipient—if that is even the correct term for a disenfranchised apartheid education—of the gratitude.

How is it even possible to conceive of gratitude—a word that comes to us from medieval Latin, *gratitudinem*, meaning "good will," "thankful," "pleasing"—in relation to an apartheid education designed to make of the disenfranchised, as offered in the Book of Joshua, "hewers of wood and drawers of water" (Joshua 9:21)? Those disenfranchised by apartheid are presented as latter-day analogues for the oppressed Gideonites who were condemned to serve the Israelites. In our turn, the disenfranchised South African majority were made to serve the apartheid masters. How, then, is it even possible to conceive of being thankful for an education designed, with great deliberation and forethought, to be inferior? The intention was to provide the disenfranchised with an education that fitted us for nothing but the most menial jobs, the most mundane tasks in a highly industrialized economy, such as apartheid South Africa boasted. The disenfranchised did most of the backbreaking work on construction sites, in factories, in public utilities; surely to recall such an experience as if it were created in the spirit of good will is nothing short of perverse. How can one "favor" or "show favor" (from the root of gratitude, *gwere*) to an apartheid education? Is to write thus, with Augustine's account of his transgression in mind, to know that "in spite of my terrors I still did wrong"?[10] Is to write thus to write "my terrors"? Perhaps that should be rephrased as to write "my errors" or to write "in error"—to write with no regard for either "my terror" or "my error."

Perversity

"Destroy" and "undo" are two of the three definitions of the twelfth-century Old French word *perverter*, from which we get "pervert," the third meaning of the medieval root of the word. As used in *The Perversity of Gratitude*, "perversity" folds "undoing" (to take apart; to reveal; to lay bare, so that to undo is always to recognize the possibility of making anew) and "destruction" (to lay waste to entirely) into one, effectively eliminating any distinction between the two meanings, all the while retaining the traces of their incompatibility.

The Perversity of Gratitude in no way accords with the hegemonic rendering of disenfranchised apartheid education—that it was bad, inferior, or, worse, barbaric. It is intolerant of this understanding not because that rendering is without merit or substance. There was a great deal about CAD education that was racist, objectionable, structurally underfunded, and unjust. That is unarguable. However, what *The Perversity of Gratitude* makes clear is that unless there is a willingness to destroy and/or undo this hegemony, it is impossible to uncover at the very (hidden) core of a CAD or BAD education precisely the conditions that made such an education ripe for thinking.

It is only through the concept of perversity that the propensity for thinking, under conditions systematically structured to militate against thinking, reveals itself as being lodged in that most unlikely of places: The very core of a CAD or BAD education. It is only through a commitment to thinking through perversity that it becomes possible to fly in the face of the governing logic, to run entirely counter to the grain of the dominant perception(s). Perversity, in this instance, is that thinking for thinking that disputes the logic of both the oppressor and the oppressed. To be perverse is to act against what is expected, what is held as a truth by almost everyone. To be perverse is to show no regard for accepted wisdom, agreed-upon understanding, and widely held beliefs. To be perverse is to refuse to kowtow to the extant epistemology. Perversity is the anthropology of thinking. Perversity is, true to its contrary nature, an unruly creature ill-disposed to subjugation. It will not subscribe to the force of history. Perversity is the commitment to think that which is presumed to be unthinkable. Perversity is a stubborn impatience with what is. Perversity is that intellectual force that undoes and destroys in the service of thinking. Perversity is the relentless determination to uncover thinking where none is said to be possible. It is only through the concept of perversity that a CAD education can be conceived of as the unintentionally ideal ground for thinking, regardless of the fact that it is an entirely incidental outcome and runs counter to the logic of the apartheid regime.

The Perversity of Gratitude:
In Three Iterations

An Argument with Myself

In creating the concept that is the perversity of gratitude, I have begun an argument that pits me against myself. It is an argument with myself in which I cannot triumph. It is an unwinnable struggle, yet it may be the most edifying struggle that I will ever undertake. It is what will, when all is said and done, keep me alive and sustain me, this struggle, this argument with myself. In the midst of this struggle, I find refuge in Derrida:

> Instead of arguing, of sending him back to this or that, I answered with a pirouette, I'll tell you, by sending him back to his question, by signifying to him that he must have been savoring, along with me, the interest he visibly was taking, at this very moment, in this question that I moreover concerned myself along with others, among them myself.[11]

This writing is nothing if not one in which I concern "myself along with others, among them myself." This question at once turns narrowly on the perversity of gratitude while never failing to open out, often into territory uncharted—a territory where there lurks who knows what. It is a treacherous question, no matter that it is absolutely a question that has already made me subject to its address. I am addressed by it directly, and because of this, I must confront the question in its polyphony. It is through his question that Derrida assigns me a task. To paraphrase him, he is sending me back to the question, signifying to me what I must have been savoring. Indeed, so urgent in its address is this question that it would be futile—to say nothing of it being utterly disingenuous—to argue against it.

Instead, what is demanded is the answer that can only emerge from the pirouette in the direction of the question about the perversity that produces, when everything else mitigates against it, a history of gratitude and an account of gratitude not least of all. This moment of which Derrida speaks belongs to that understanding of time that extends beyond any mere comprehension of time as temporal. What constitutes temporality in this instance is to understand that time that cannot be grasped through the ticking of a clock; the act of watching the hands on a wristwatch move in a series of inexorable circles will not suffice here. It is not a date that can be marked on a calendar or that marks a beginning (say, 1948) or an end (say, 1990 or 1994).

No, this Derridean moment is best apprehended in terms of what historians call the *longue durée*. It extends across chronology even as it refuses to abide by that clock named "history"—that clock according to which one mode of structural organization precedes another, one mode of structural organization is displaced by another. As such, this moment constitutes an epoch, a conception of time as organized around an event, and in this case, that event is apartheid. Here, apartheid is that event through which we come to know the time that was as manifesting itself in the trace. Apartheid is the all-too-legible inscription that will not abide by the logic of historic triumph—the overcoming of apartheid. It is the time that will not subscribe to the political terms of its successor, "postapartheid"; the past has been—or is being—made obsolete by the forces of the present. Apartheid, conceptualized as the perversity of gratitude, stands against any easy transition to its temporal and, in some ways, structurally distinct successor, postapartheid. The thinking that is the perversity of gratitude is the stubborn, indefatigable resistance of the historically disenfranchised to the educational structure and political ethos of the present. The perversity of gratitude is the legible inscription of an indestructible past that makes visible the all-too-present traces of apartheid that persist into the putative time after. To proclaim fidelity to the perversity of gratitude is to throw the entire edifice of postapartheid South Africa into question.

The event of apartheid is the trace that lingers into the time that is. Like all the great catastrophes in history, the trace is resistant to absolute destruction. (The event of apartheid here presents itself as the time that still is. It refuses all arguments to the contrary, so assured is its self-positioning.) It is that time we can always discern, no matter the effort we expend in laying it waste. It is an understanding of time that is uncanny in its ability to present itself to us in the least expected and most inopportune moments. It is a moment with which Derrida, in his meditation on the Shoah, is intimate and familiar, coming to him as it did in a single, ghostly, phrase. Derrida writes, "It imposed itself upon me with the authority, so discreet and simple it was, of a judgment: 'cinders there are' (*il y a là cendre*). . . . I had to explain myself to it, respond to it—or for it."[12] Out of the indestructibility that is cinders and ashes, that is how this time must be written. Barely discernible, indefatigably visible. Inscrutable, demanding to be written. To demand to be written is to insist upon thinking everything that remains of, and in, the cinders and ashes. Through cinders, this time that must be thought "imposes itself upon me with the authority, so discreet and simple it was, of a judgment." It that time to which we must "explain ourselves," to which we must "respond." It is a time that holds us responsible for it. A time we can only begin to think by giving ourselves to it. In giving ourselves to it we take the first step in explaining ourselves to it. And in explaining ourselves, the raw, bare, outlines of that time's self-explication reveals itself to us. As though it were a gift.

It is the time that we know all too well as the time that haunts us. It makes us out of joint with our contemporary. This time not only jars us loose from the contemporary, it sets us adrift. No matter our effort to lay it to rest, this time disturbs our sleep and is the source of an irrepressible discomfort in our waking hours. It is the time in which we came to be but that remains, for all its maternal propensities, a perpetual source of comfort that is eternally hostile to us. It is the time that will not ever leave us alone. It will never let us be without intruding upon us, always demanding that we think the perversity of gratitude, and we cannot refuse. It reminds us that we are called upon to think because the perversity of gratitude is, like no other time, *our* time. This is the only time that is truly ours, the only time in—and to—which we truly belong. And yet it is a time we cannot lay claim to even as it is that time that has taken us into its possession. It is a time to which we have, unbeknownst to us, long since given ourselves up to, willingly. It constitutes us. It is the time against which we can mount no attack without risking ourselves in the process. It gives us life even as it holds us hostage. It is the time we vigorously resist (a futile act) and to which we sometimes gladly submit, giving ourselves over in order to be ourselves. It is a time in which we can be ourselves as we understand ourselves to be.

It is a time to which we can, now, in our reckoning with it and because of accounting for ourselves in relation to it, append the proper noun we already invoked. It is a possessive time, and as such, it is a time that will not tolerate an affinity for any other times. It insists, this time, that it must be addressed and known by only one name: The perversity of gratitude.

Despite ourselves, the perversity of gratitude is a time for which we long. It is a time to which we are and always will be drawn. We long to possess that time so that we might be able to possess ourselves in that time, even as we know full well that such possession will always be beyond us. It is a time, we would say incorrectly, for which we are nostalgic—nostalgic in the way that Jacques Lacan renders mourning, which is the irretrievable loss of a love object that seems impossible to live without. The love object here is the loss of a disenfranchised education.

In its temporality, the perversity of gratitude constitutes an intensely politicized form of mourning. It is perverse, of course, in that it is the historically disenfranchised struggling to reconcile themselves to the loss of a time—disenfranchised apartheid education—that the present insists should be condemned to the past. How could the disenfranchised mourn the time of their subjugation? How could the historically disenfranchised be nostalgic for their apartheid education? How is it possible that such a longing for what was be constituted out of an apparently unending gratitude?

The perversity of gratitude irrupts the present because it speaks the truth of an unspeakable and unbreakable attachment to *that* moment the present insists must be eschewed and is intent on denying. It is the moment the present demands must be given up to the oblivion of history. The present must live at a remove from it by rupturing itself from that time in which the perversity of gratitude came to be.

In its irruptive, disruptive enduring, the perversity of gratitude bears testimony to the impossibility of laying waste to that time. The perversity of gratitude is that time undoes all those formed by and in it into earlier, resolute, unwelcome, hospitable, hostile, self-annihilating, self-affirming iterations of themselves—the only self to which the 1976 generation, rendered metonymically, can be true.

The perversity of gratitude is that time cautioned us, long in advance—a caution history demanded we ignore—against what was *l'avenir* (what was to come).

The perversity of gratitude stands, even now, in this late moment, as a warning against what is to come.

It is a warning to which insufficient heed was paid. It is a warning that persists into the contemporary because, at its core, the perversity of gratitude contains an impregnable truth.

The perversity of gratitude is the time of thinking—the time that permits nothing but *das Denken denken*.

The perversity of gratitude is the interdict against nostalgia (mourning) that owes everything to that time it is determined, against itself, to remember—that time in which the perversity of gratitude, in moments of complete honesty, enjoins those whom it holds in its thrall to rejoice and to proclaim their fidelity to that perversity of gratitude. It is that moment for which those who came to be in that perverse time understand themselves to be, in a word, eternally grateful.

The Perversity of Rwandan Gratitude

A Rwandan colleague, at a very pleasant dinner during a conference on African philosophy in a rather charming New England college town a few years ago, made me sit up and take notice. She roused me from my meal when she said something about being grateful to Paul Kgame.

The colleague in question is a survivor of the genocide. As a Hutu, she had been subjected to horrendous violence by the Tutsis. This included experiencing near starvation, destitution, and the death of family members and having been a witness to rapes. The first question that comes to mind is, naturally, the one that registers utter incomprehensibility: How could gratitude be extended to a leader who oversaw such violence, who wreaked such devastation on the people of Rwanda and on the entire Great Lakes region? Her answer, singular in its force, could not be mistaken. Her voice, though slightly tremulous, clearly reflected her sense of political accuracy, of gratitude. "He saved the country." At whose expense, I wondered? There are none so blind as those who will not see; none so inured to what is being presented to them as those who will not hear.

Still, in the face of her gratitude to Kgame, my incredulity grew. I found myself unable to let it go, to bow to the severity, to imagine what it must be to live with such pain and to know the self as inordinately complicit with terror, as we all are, in one way or another. Does any sociopolitical construct have the right to ask this of us? Out of my struggle with her gratitude, I retorted: "You have made a deal with the devil, and the devil always gets his due." Make no mistake, the devil gets what's due to him. That is arguably the most enduring lesson of history—maybe, maybe. In my retort, there is, as is surely clear, a constitutive self-indictment. What due have I afforded—am I affording, through this writing—the devil that was my apartheid education?

Perversity, in the Fashion of St. Paul

The Protestant Revolution, Karl Marx points out, was spearheaded by Martin Luther, who "donned the mask of the Apostle Paul." In their turn, the revolutionaries of 1848 (those subjects of Marx's *1848 Manuscripts*) were in the debt of the "revolutionary tradition of 1793 to 1795."[13] Every tradition—certainly every tradition that has produced an event—is marked by the trace of some other event in history, but only if we take history to be composed of a series of revolutionary events (the French Revolution, the Enlightenment, the Industrial Revolution, the many and varied struggles for national sovereignty, etc.). We revisit Marx's essay in the next interlude. For now, however, let us attend to the ways in which language is borrowed here.

This language—the one in which this writing is enacted—is not mine. I cannot claim it as mine. It is, rather, borrowed from nowhere else than the history of apartheid. Let us allow the moment—history, if you will—to decide whether or not ours is an "epoch of revolutionary crisis."[14] There can, however, be no doubt that it is Marx's spirit that guides this writing because the tradition under which this address came to be is weighed down by the past; it is a writing freighted with and steeped in the past.

The tradition of which Marx speaks, the hauntology that is the spirit of Soweto 1976, comes into presence in *The Perversity of Gratitude*.

As Marx points out, Martin Luther had no compunction about borrowing from the political modality of that most radical apostle, St. Paul. Those who are of the Christological persuasion need no reminding, of course, that Paul is singular among the Apostles precisely because he was not present at the event. Peter, Matthew, Mark, Luke, and John were all there. Every one of the disciples witnessed the crucifixion. It does not matter that they doubted on that early Sunday morning that the figure before them was the risen Jesus the Christ; it remains only to be said that they were present.

Paul, alone among the Apostles, was not party to the event, so his faith was always of a greater intensity. He believed, all the more zealously—which lent him an imperious cast of mind and a politics no less imperial in its practice—because he was not present. That is among the reasons why Paul was such an exemplary figure of thought for Luther. Paul was impatient with Peter's politesse and his ability to negotiate the demands of building a church and establishing political order in Jerusalem and Rome. But the extension of the Church to Antioch, to Asia Minor, to the Greeks, paving the way for St. James in the Iberian Peninsula, was the work of the evangelical zealot Paul. And unlike Peter, who was first and foremost dedicated to pastoring his newly minted flock, Paul was a man of letters. In the New Testament, it is Paul's letters that speak of proselytization, of spreading the faith north, east, and still farther east. It is Paul who is best able to testify to the event of the crucifixion and the resurrection precisely because he is the figure of faith in Christianity; he was not there, and still he believed. Only he could spread the Gospel, could speak with authority, because while he was not present at the event, he was drawn into the circle of faith in the wake of the event and entirely transformed by it. Paul alone was testament to the effect of faith. He testified to that, in the face of all kinds of historical oppositions from the Jews of Jerusalem and the animists of Asia Minor. Paul was a threat to the established epistemological order as much as he presented a radical challenge to Peter's Church in Rome.

No wonder, then, that it is Paul, not Peter or John (the inaugural baptismal figure), who preoccupies philosophers. Paul alone speaks from the place of *ecriture*, of writing—and, as such, writing as the place and as the mode of thinking. *Logos* means "word"—the Word, the first word. It is no wonder, then, that every major thinker in the Christian tradition, from Augustine to Luther, engages Paul, or, in the latter's case, takes political cues from him. It is little surprise that in the early to mid-2000s, Paul again showed himself as the most trusted and venerable friend of philosophers. St. Paul was, once more, back in vogue. In truth, St. Paul is never out of vogue, certainly not for very long.

Giorgio Agamben (*The Time That Remains*),[15] Alain Badiou (*Saint Paul: The Foundation of Universalism*),[16] and Slavoj Žižek (*The Puppet and the Dwarf: The Perverse Core of Christianity*)[17] all, in the same historical instant, turned their attention to that prolific man of letters, that inveterate proselytizer. (In 1993, Jacob Taubes published *Die Politische Theologie des Paulus—The Political Theology of Paul*,[18] translated and published in English in 2004; so Taubes's work both antedates—anticipates—and belongs to the same movement of that most recent Pauline revival since all of the works are published in a two year span, 2003–2005.)

It is Žižek, however, whose Pauline writing is of most interest here because the Slovenian philosopher presents perversity as a radical political act. In brief, Žižek argues that the crucial figure in the Christian faith, at least as it pertains to the event, is that most despised disciple, Judas Iscariot. Without Judas's betrayal, there can be no crucifixion; without the crucifixion, there can be no resurrection; and without the resurrection, there can be, of course, no promise of eternal life. Nothing less than transcendence is what the sacrifice that is Jesus the Christ's crucifixion guarantees. The perverse core of Christianity, then, derives from Judas's betrayal.

It is not faith but a failure of earth-shattering proportion, almost literally, that secures the everlasting life that Christianity promises. This is to say that perversity must not, in the terms of the event, be either condemned or dismissed. We do so at our peril.

Perversity must instead be brought into presence as the very condition for thinking. The radical kernel, truth itself, may be found in perversity. In Žižek's Pauline formulation of the event, it is (only) through perversity that we can hope to gain access to truth. It is only through acknowledging betrayal as a philosophical fundament that we can achieve salvation; only because of betrayal does salvation become possible. All followers of Jesus the Christ are indebted to Judas Iscariot. Without Judas's betrayal, Jesus the Christ would have remained a charismatic local preacher who was active around Galilee and surrounded by a core of committed adherents—hardly the stuff of an earth-shattering messianism or any different from scores of other preachers in Galilee, Bethlehem, and Jerusalem, where there were many of Jesus the Christ's ilk. No wonder Badiou locates in Paul the "foundation of universalism."[19]

More power, then, to a Pauline-inspired betrayal. Out of Pauline betrayal emerges a new ground for thinking—for thinking perversity, for thinking out of the conditions that only perversity can bring into being. What philosophical good is gratitude if it does not contain within it a radical kernel that can be taken up to think the radical propensities lodged in a CAD education that is now, contrary to its original intent, presented as fertile ground for thinking?

Against Commonsense

If we follow this line of thinking, it becomes possible to understand how the perversity of gratitude confounds the political common-sense of apartheid, particularly if we take commonsense to be the stuff of everyday logic, the rationale, the expectations of the apartheid regime, the outcomes that the ruling National Party (NP) government anticipated its policies would achieve. By refusing this logic, the perversity of gratitude draws the very notion of commonsense itself into question. As thinkers have long argued, Heidegger and Stuart Hall among them, commonsense (what Heidegger designates, in a most provocative and counterintuitive instantiation, "Gerege," meaning "idle talk"[20]) is not at all common. That presumed mode of being in the world is neither common (ordinary, self-explicatory, as Heidegger reminds us) nor free of artifice. Commonsense is, as Hall shows us, the outcome of ideological production. In his argument, Hall follows the work of Antonio Gramsci, drawing especially on Gramsci's notion of hegemony. Following Gramsci, there is no such mode of apprehension that can be named, in the sense that we now understand it, "commonsense." That which we name "common" and take to be so obvious as to not require any explication must itself be made subject to thinking.

A remarkably perverse place from which to embark upon the thinking of an apartheid education is to willfully set out against that which is expected. Whereas the predominant (anti-apartheid and post-apartheid) disposition is toward the denunciation of a CAD or BAD education, there is no such condemnation to be found here. Instead, in its place is a thinking that is disposed not to denunciation but to gratitude. Such an argument can, of course, only proceed—if it is to succeed—by obstinately, informed as it is by the requisite assiduousness and care (such an argument must be tended to, taken into the self's care), resisting all commonsense. The perversity of gratitude must fly in the face of extant presumptions about what is "good," "correct," "right," especially as these terms pertain to the hegemonic understanding of anti- and postapartheid politics. Thinking the perversity of gratitude begins, for this very reason, by turning its face from all such hegemonic—"commonsense"—presumptions.

It locates the good in the wrong place and in the wrong—oppressive, repressive, authoritarian, racist—institutions. It makes such a determination, as we are now aware, because it unconceals a clearing in which autoimmunity is, contrary to all expectation, the prevailing philosophical condition. In this clearing, what takes place can only be named "thinking."

Because it is so dead set against the commonsense of apartheid, anti-apartheid, and the persistence of that commonsense in the milieu that is postapartheid South Africa, the perversity of gratitude must, perforce, assume a cantankerous, logic-defying mood.

There is a perverse agreement between the architects, enforcers, and beneficiaries of apartheid and its opponents and victims. Also perverse is the fact that the positions of the apartheid regime and of anti-apartheid activists echo and reinforce each other without, as far as is known, a requisite thinking of their coinciding. The logic of inferior education is accepted as dogma in apartheid South Africa before hardening into an unarguable truth in postapartheid society. *The Perversity of Gratitude* works, in a range of registers, to destroy this axiom—For good reason.

To restore gratitude, in relation to perversity, it is necessary to "go back there." This makes it possible to "unconceal" (*alētheaia*)— to bring into truth—that which can only come to light through destruction. (For Heidegger, "concealment preserves what is most proper to *alētheaia* [truth] as its own."[21]) In this way, "destruction" clears or opens the path to thinking, and that path must always be alert to that which is "most proper to concealment." *Alētheaia*, that which is most proper to concealment, as it pertains to a CAD education, is thinking. To unconceal what is most proper to concealment is to begin to lay bare that which has remained concealed—that which has not yet been thought and must now be thought.

It is under these circumstances that, in writing *The Perversity of Gratitude*, I "come back" to Cape Town, much as I no longer wish to return, much as I have long since found it impossible to leave. I come back to the classrooms of Livingstone High School, back to the lecture halls of UWC, back to the rude jumble of life that was Hanover Park, the working-class township where I came of age.

I come back, then, not to contemporary Cape Town but to apartheid-era Cape Town, the site of my elementary, high school, and undergraduate education. Apartheid-era Cape Town is where I belonged to the ranks of the disenfranchised; it is the place of my very first thinking. It is to this place that I trace the perversity of my gratitude. What must be brought out of concealment? Why has it remained so long in concealment? Can *alēthaeia* only emerge out of the unconcealment that is the perversity of gratitude? To come back is to know that coming back is inconceivable, in Žižek's argument, without Judas Iscariot's perversity.

The perverse truth, then, is that I have thrown in my lot with Judas Iscariot's without reservation or apology. I have chosen the company of the most famous betrayer in Christianity and maybe the most famous—and reviled?—betrayer in all of monotheism.

I have done this on the philosophical premise that betrayal is fecund ground for thinking.

To betray on the order of Judas Iscariot is to know betrayal as the gateway to thinking.

Such is the perverse logic of the perversity of gratitude.

I

A Name: Livingstone High School

Richard Owen Dudley: 1924–2009

Nulla Vestiga Retrosum. (The school motto: "No footsteps backward.")

Yeobright loved his kind. He had a conviction that the want of most men was knowledge of a sort which brings wisdom rather than affluence.

—**Thomas Hardy,** *The Return of the Native*

To be a disenfranchised pupil made to think by and because of apartheid was to know Marxist contingency of "The Eighteenth Brumaire of Louis Bonaparte" variety. In this essay, about whose contents we already have an inkling, Marx is sly but merciless in his mockery of Louis Bonaparte's ineptitude and pretentiousness. Marx writes:

> Men make their own history, but they do not make it under circumstances chosen by themselves, but under circumstances directly found, given and transmitted from the past. The tradition of all the dead generation weighs like a nightmare on the brain of the living. And just when they seem engaged in revolutionizing themselves and things, in creating something entirely new, precisely in such epochs of revolutionary crisis they anxiously conjure up spirits of the past to their service and borrow from them names, battle slogans and costumes in order to present the new scene of world history in this time-honored guise and this borrowed language.[1]

The past and the present were the "circumstance" of apartheid, and it was against—and despite—this nightmarish weight that an anti-apartheid pedagogy was forged (and had to be forged) at institutions such as Livingstone.

However, what the CAD authorities had no way of reckoning with was Livingstone's own traditions, developed, burnished, renewed, and maintained over several generations, both living and dead. In no way could CAD, whose creation Richard Owen Dudley, I. B. Tabata, and others in their political and pedagogical circle fervently opposed (an opposition which saw Dudley join the anti-CAD movement), account for a figure such as Richard Owen Dudley. To the Livingstone student body, Mr. Dudley was more popularly known as R. O. or Pops (the latter of which was a name used only out of earshot). He was the Livingstone vice principal during my tenure at the school and filled in as the acting principal for the principal, Mr. Evans, when he was on leave. To his friends, R. O. was "Dick."

R. O. quite literally instantiated Livingstone. He has the distinction of being the school's most eminent figure, but he was also the only teacher who had emerged fully through the institution's ranks.

Mr. Dudley was not only himself a Livingstone alum; he belonged to Livingstone's first graduating class. That is no mean feat. It is, however, made all the more remarkable by the fact that he did so at the age of fifteen. R. O. had arrived at Livingstone from St. Andrew's Mission School, where his father, Samuel, was the principal. (The young Richard had started primary school at the tender age of four.) After Livingstone, where he was the head boy[2] (it almost goes without saying), R. O. entered UCT. He started at UCT in 1939 and graduated in 1945, now possessed of bachelor of science and master of science degrees, together with a teacher's diploma. A few months before Mr. Dudley died, he was awarded an honorary doctorate from his alma mater.[3]

By some accounts, R. O. enjoyed the proceedings, which were conducted at his bedside. To me, however, no conferring of a Ph.D. could in any way elevate Mr. Dudley. His status as a teacher who taught thinking in no way relied on institutional accreditation. He thought because of who he was, not because of the letters that preceded or succeeded his name. "R. O." or "Mr. Dudley" would do as well, if we allow for the honorific "Mr." (or "Ms.," or "Mrs.") that was universally applied to all teachers in South Africa. The affectionate "Pops" was always sufficient for me, and then some. He was a thinking man. He was an intellectual. That was enough.[4]

R. O. began teaching physics, mathematics, and English (the last of which only for a year) at Livingstone when he was twenty. Uniquely positioned thus, R. O. was a singular figure. He was himself a beneficiary, curator, and daily transmitter of Livingstone's "traditions." A tradition so uniquely embodied did, indeed, weigh heavily on the institution, but mainly it assumed the form of responsibility to the institution's understanding of itself as a bastion of thinking. That place where the work of the intellect could be traced to the past but remained an active and ongoing enterprise in the present, with the present always as guardian of the past and incubator for what was to come. As a force of transmission, Livingstone's traditions instilled in every successive generation a keen sense of what it meant to be heirs to such an institutional, pedagogical, intellectual, and political history. As generation after generation of students passed through Livingstone's hallways, our ties to the historical and political substance of the institution bound us to it in perpetuity—a perpetuity that, as the school song promises, transcends any geographical remove and makes nothing of diasporization:

> We may roam the wide world over
> We may scale the highest peak
> But we always will remember
> The school whose aim has been
> *Nulla vestiga retrosum*
> Whose name we hold in high esteem

To travel the world and still be felicitous in our relationship to it and to know, upon the moment of first setting foot at 100 Lansdowne Road, that one would be allowed "no footsteps backward" is to also know the truth of that relationship.

When the class of 1980, my class, entered the institution in January 1976, we were made acutely aware of our responsibility to the institution from the very first moment. In February 1976, Livingstone celebrated its fiftieth anniversary. For our troubles as entering freshmen ("Standard Sixes,"[5] we were called), we sat through a two-hour (I would not bet against it being three; to a teenager, it seemed like an eternity) lecture by R. O. Livingstone's oracle was speaking, and no one interrupts a school's éminence grise. (A little like Fidel Castro did when giving speeches, R. O. could go on. That his lectures did not stretch to eight hours was a mercy to us, although I suspect that R. O. had a Fidel marathon in him.)

Richard Owen Dudley was a physics teacher, a political activist who had been imprisoned by the regime in the 1960s, and, more than anything else, a man of the Book. I and many others can attest that he read voraciously and expansively but always discriminately. His was the world of ideas, in no way circumscribed by discipline. He sought, as Thomas Hardy's Yeobright does, "knowledge of a sort that brings wisdom" and would abide no disciplinary strictures.

I imagined that I knew the depth of his knowledge during my Livingstone days, but I was wrong. I would, however, come to know the truth of his knowledge more intimately in the decades that followed. That R. O. read Raymond Williams, a leading figure of the New Left in Britain, would later prove a matter of intellectual significance for me. I know that he was familiar with Williams, that son of the Welsh border country, in Williams's telling, because on a dreary late-winter's day in August 1979, R. O. quizzed my class (9B, Mrs. MacArthur's class) with a question. I remember that question so well I can almost recount exactly where R. O. was standing when he posed it: "What is culture?" We tried our level best, aspiring to rarefied heights ("Classical," we ventured; "Beethoven," someone suggested—wrong, all wrong), but the answer, as all cultural studies scholars know (and knew already by the mid-1950s), is, well, sort of obvious: "Ordinary." That is what "culture" is, R. O. informed us, thereby not only putting us out of our misery but sowing, at least in my case, the seeds of my later work.

During my second semester as a graduate student at Columbia University in New York City, I would read that Raymond Williams essay, "Culture Is Ordinary." It is an extraordinary essay, beautiful in its simplicity but above all lyrical. It is an essay redolent with *feeling*, that word that is given affective force and depth by Williams in his concept, the "structure of feeling." (In truth, it is one of the great strengths of Williams's work that he is able to make us feel that which we think. Nowhere is this more true for me than in *Culture & Society*.) Ostensibly a series of observations gleaned while on a bus ride, Williams's essay really captures the rhythms of the working-class life in south Wales—the life that is the history of his family, a reflection on the place where he came of age. The first three paragraphs of "Culture Is Ordinary" could easily stand as *the* Welsh bildungsroman of the postwar working-class variety. I quote his work at some length, such is the beauty of Williams's prose—a beauty that is not offset, I hope, by my parsing of it. The parsing itself stands as less a gratuitous editorializing and more a Dudleyesque interruption, with me breaking in at those moments when Mr. Dudley's perspicuity presents itself most saliently to me:

> The bus stop was outside the Cathedral. I had been looking at the Mappa Mundi with its rivers out of Paradise, and at the chained library, where a party of clergymen had got in easily but where I had waited an hour and cajoled a verger before I even got to see the chains. Now, across the street, a cinema advertised the *Six-Five Special* and a cartoon version of *Gulliver's Travels*. The bus arrived, with a driver and a conductress deeply absorbed in each other. We went out of the city, over the old bridge, and on through the orchards and the green meadows and the fields red under the plough.[6]

Williams is lyrical about the landscape, drawing us into his familiarity with it, detailing its particularities, sharing his sensibility of the place with us:

> Ahead were the Black Mountains, and we climbed among them, watching the steep fields end at the grey walls, beyond which the bracken and heather and whin had not yet been driven back. To the east, along the ridge, stood the line of grey Norman castles; to the west, the fortress wall of the mountains. Then, as we still climbed, the rock changed under us. Here, now, was limestone,

and the line of the early iron workings along the scarp. The farming valleys, with their scattered white houses, fell away behind. Ahead of us were the narrower valleys: the steel-rolling mill, the gasworks, the grey terraces, the pitheads. The bus stopped, and the driver and conductress got out, still absorbed. They had done this journey so often, and seen all its stages. It is a journey, in fact, that in one form or another we have all made.[7]

This journey we have just now made with Williams takes in the topography of the place as it catalogues the economy of the region—the "steel-rolling mills, the gasworks . . . the pitheads." Williams sees these mills and mines as integral to the landscape, not yet the ecological catastrophes that we will later come to know (i.e., the deleterious effects of the pollution caused by the steel mills and the dangers posed by plumbing the depths of the earth through mining). These industries are, for Williams, simply modes of being that sustain—and have sustained, for generations—those with whom he is now sharing a bus ride:

> I was born and grew up halfway along that bus journey. Where I lived is still a farming valley, though the road through it is being widened and straightened, to carry the heavy lorries to the north. Not far away, my grandfather, and so back through the generations, worked as a farm labourer until he was turned out of his cottage and, in his fifties, became a roadman. His sons went at thirteen or fourteen on to the farms, his daughters into service. My father, his third son, left the farm at fifteen to be a boy porter on the railway, and later became a signalman, working in a box in this valley until he died.[8]

Williams would immortalize his railway signalman father in his novel *Border Country*. The son of a working-class Welshman, Williams graduated from Cambridge University and went on to help found the field of cultural studies, a critical mode of contemporary thinking. It all started in that Welsh village:

I went up the road to the village school, where a curtain divided the two classes—Second to eight or nine, First to fourteen. At eleven I went to the local grammar school, and later to Cambridge.

Culture is ordinary: that is where we must start. To grow up in that country was to see the shape of a culture, and its modes of change. I could stand on the mountains and look north to the farms and the cathedral, or south to the smoke and flare of the blast furnace making a second sunset.[9]

In the shadow of industrialism, domestic intellectual ferment was the order of the day in the Williams household:

To grow up in that family was to see the shaping of minds: the learning of new skills, the shifting of relationships, the emergence of different language and ideas. My grandfather, a big hard labourer, wept while he spoke, finely and excitedly, at the parish meeting, of being turned out of his cottage. My father, not long before he died, spoke quietly and happily of when he had started a trade-union branch and a Labour Party group in the village, and, without bitterness, of the "kept men" of the new politics. I speak a different idiom, but I think of these same things.[10]

All of Williams's reflections culminate in and are punctuated by an assertion that attained a historic memorability for me—a singular pronouncement, a declaration that broke open a world for me: "Culture is ordinary: that is the first fact."[11]

Williams, the grandson of a man who had known deracination—the experience of "being turned out of his cottage"—looked at the Hereford Mappa Mundi, that medieval map of the world housed in the Hereford Cathedral, which dates to the fourteenth century. Reading "Culture Is Ordinary" just a stone's throw from an elite U.S. university, on New York's Upper West Side, I thrilled to Williams's essay. His trajectory from village grammar school to the halls of Cambridge resonated with me. His "different idiom" suggested, in a language distilled to its poetic essence, that it was possible to produce my own idiom, one that could bear the weight of my thinking. After all, I too knew laborers, and disenfranchised South Africa—Livingstone in particular—was a cauldron of radical politics, much like the Welsh Labour Party groups were. If Williams's father was tolerant of the type of "kept men" that the "new politics" threw up, R. O. was not, because he warned us against all manner of kept men. His warning sometimes took the form of an impish dismissal, but it was a warning all the same. I regret to say that despite R. O.'s best efforts, out of my generation at Livingstone would emerge a few kept men and women who immersed themselves fully in the new postapartheid politics. It served them well, at least in material terms. But, always, R.O.'s judgment will hover above them. An indictment that has no need to pronounce itself.

For our part, in standard 10, we were becoming familiar with the ways that marked and the protagonists who peopled the Wessex landscape of Hardy's fiction. Our prescribed fiction for that year was Hardy's *Tess of the d'Urbervilles*, a novel that acquainted us with stolid, dependable farmer Gabriel Oak and the titular Tess, a landowner's daughter unable to resist the charms of the itinerant Angel Clare. An insubstantial figure of late nineteenth-century English masculinity, Clare lacks heft in general but certainly in comparison to Oak. Drifting through Wessex (a landscape conjured out of Hardy's native Dorset and the surrounding counties), Clare has no autochthonous relationship to the land. He is an opportunist, a lothario passing by and seducing Tess, who is an easy mark for Angel's big-city wiles. In outline, if not in particular, Yeobright was a figure not unfamiliar to us.

Like Hardy's Yeobright and Gabriel Oak, R. O. sought something other than affluence. He sought to instill in us a desire for something with greater intellectual and ethical heft. He offered us a prophylactic against materialism and power. R. O. interdicted us to resist the temptations of Mammon. Affluence—the acquisition of capital and influence—for its own sake did not sit well with R. O. It diminishes the human spirit, R. O. hinted subtly but never moralistically, making of the "new men" empty husks not to be emulated.

For R. O., to know culture as ordinary was to acknowledge the integrity and value of our everyday lived experience. It was to show regard for the communities out of which we had emerged. It was, in relation to Livingstone, to give credence to the extraordinariness of an intellectual culture that fortified us against the onslaught of the apartheid state, its many functionaries, its violence, and all those institutions through which it exercised power.

While reading "Culture Is Ordinary" in 1990, I was returned to that day in August 1979, when R. O. posed that question. Once again, no matter that he was eight thousand miles away, I found myself held in his thrall. Having lived with his question for more than a decade, I had happened upon the answer in an institution very different from the one in which I had first encountered the question. The mark of true pedagogy is that it adheres to no timetable. The effects of true pedagogy cannot be measured by examination results. It does not show up in a report card. It is, rather, a gift on the order of a bequest. It is a question that we must, at some point or other, confront and, whether or not we consider ourselves prepared for it, answer. Such a question, in its persistence, is what makes us accountable to thinking. The truth of the question cannot be stayed, at least not indefinitely. The power of the question is that it will not leave us be. It assumes a ghostly afterlife, even as we "roam the wide world over."

True pedagogy is that assertion, that provocation, or, as is infinitely more likely, that insight, in the moment of its being presented, that unsettles, disturbs, and discomfits the student. It haunts the student, not only for days or weeks after, but for years—decades, in my case. I would, fifteen years after that question, complete a dissertation that figured as intellectuals not only C.L.R. James and Stuart Hall (who ranks foremost among cultural studies scholars and worked alongside Williams and Richard Hoggart) but Muhammad Ali and Bob Marley too. True pedagogy is not, in its most efficacious and provocative articulation, punctual. It adheres, rather, like the logic of the event, to its own timetable. It presents itself in its own good time. True pedagogy is, in a word, Socratic. It is the question the teacher gives the student so as to make out of the student one who thinks—thinks the question, thinks the first iteration of the question—and, most importantly, it is the question that bears within itself the very germs of (a) thinking.

In and with my dissertation, I was doing nothing more than answering R. O.'s question. More than that, even, the question had fomented in me to the point of a post-Gramscian articulation. If Antonio Gramsci insisted in his famous essay "On Intellectuals" that "all men are intellectuals,"[12] I had, inspired by R. O., formulated my own answer. In response to Gramsci's democratization of the intellectual, which has given us the term "organic intellectual," I argued for Ali and Marley, as well as James and Hall, as "vernacular intellectuals."

My dissertation, I can now say, has a specific birth date: August 1979. It has a specific site: Mrs. MacArthur's class, room 9, Livingstone High School. My dissertation was born in apartheid-era Cape Town, far from where it was written, in a tiny apartment on New York City's Lower East Side. It was born long before I knew of its coming into being. It was present, incipiently so, even as I was unaware of it. Long before I became aware of it, my preoccupation with intellectuals and thinking was already presenting itself to me. It was presenting itself in such a manner as Fredric Jameson describes in taking up the "problem of acts" in Sartre's work. "The future act," Jameson writes, "the totally new, already exists in an ill-formed manner in the present."[13] My future act, as I can now attest, no matter that it was ill-formed, is what I subsequently transformed out of that long-ago present—a present that has shown itself to be my all-defining line of intellectual inquiry.

At long last, I was able to answer R. O.'s question. In truth, I was able to answer the question not because it became present to me, but rather, as Heidegger would have it, because I became present to it. I had indeed let the question be, as Heidegger advises, but I became present to the question in no small measure because it would not let me be.

I came to know that "culture is ordinary." And so, at long last, I was able to answer R. O.'s question, courtesy of the path opened up for me by his familiarity with Williams's most famous essay. It is an essay, together with Williams's *Culture & Society*, Richard Hoggart's *The Uses of Literacy*, and E. P. Thompson's *The Making of the English Working Class*, that forms the basis of the field that would become cultural studies. (James's *Beyond a Boundary* would, in later articulations of cultural studies, become an important supplement to Williams's, Hoggart's, and Thompson's work.) Cultural studies is a field shaped by, among other forces, three events that took place in 1956. Most importantly, perhaps, there was Nikita Khrushchev's denunciation of Stalinism, as well as the Suez crisis and the Soviet invasion of Hungary. The historic failure that was Stalinism produced a generation of thinkers (in the British New Left, Hall as much, or maybe even more than, any other) determined to renovate Marxism, to make of it a mode of thinking and being freed from historic atrocity—Stalin's gulags and purges being primary among those motivating factors.

For his part, R. O. knew his Marx and was familiar with James's oeuvre. Like intellectuals enamored of James, R. O. favored James's *The Black Jacobins: Toussaint L'Ouverture and the San Domingo Revolution*.[14] I incline, and then not slightly, in the direction of *Beyond a Boundary*, much as I too was influenced early by James's account of the San Domingue revolution. It is, however, the centrality of cricket and literature to *Beyond A Boundary*—"Thackeray, not Marx," James announces, with a touch of his characteristic hubris, "bears the heaviest responsibility for me"[15]—and the grappling with the promise and the cost of diasporic life that tilt things in the direction of *Beyond a Boundary* for me.

Unusual for a man of his class (educated and middle class but by no means middlebrow), the popular was a subject of consideration for Mr. Dudley. Knowing this, it becomes easy to say that Williams's line of argument about the "ordinariness of culture" made sense for R. O. Those who shared Mr. Dudley's (race and) class status (mainly other middle-class coloureds, though by no means exclusively) venerated what they took to be "high culture." In these circles, an elite bookishness reigned, derived directly from the reification of formal education—that is, academic qualifications, of which many in this intelligentsia, to be fair, boasted their fair share. (Many of them were teachers, with a sprinkling of medical professionals, lawyers, and the odd small businessperson.) No one could claim, however, that this version of coloured middle-class bookishness was entirely devoid of its own snobbishness. Its cultural predilections (superiority, some would say, and not without justification) made this class unremarkable in history. The petite bourgeoisie is, everywhere in history, a class benighted by its insubstantial pretensions.[16]

It was out of this social and ideological milieu, during the war years, that the Non-European Unity Movement (NEUM), more commonly known as simply the Unity Movement, emerged. Shaped by Enlightenment thinking, the Unity Movement was founded in 1943 by intellectuals such as Dudley, Benny and Helen Kies, and Tabata and advocated a Ten Point Program based on the concept of noncollaboration with the apartheid state. The Ten Point Program, by itself a fascinating ideological document, proposed the Unity Movement's vision of a nonracial society. (It is ironic, then, no matter that it is historically explicable, that the NEUM should take as central to its name the extant racial categorization "Non-European"—a categorization, it must be said, that predated formal apartheid. The then-ruling United Party, which would be defeated by the NP in the 1948 elections, had a less stringent racial policy, but under the United Party government, led by internationally venerated statesman Jan Smuts, South Africa was still a racially segregated society.)

Acutely aware of how racism and antisemitism had brought about the catastrophe that was World War II, the Unity Movement bound itself to the Enlightenment principle of an inherent human equality, with the inalienable right to liberty and, true as the Unity Movement was to the spirit of the French Revolution, the franchise; it is the extension of the French Revolution to San Domingue, in which Toussaint L'Ouverture played the leading role, which James documents so lyrically, that made *The Black Jacobins* so fundamental a text to R. O. and his colleagues. The Unity Movement's founding premise, however, was the negation of race[17]—the absolute refusal of any biological difference within humanity, bar what they deemed to be superficial distinctions in, say, varying levels of melanin or hair texture.

Committed antifascists that they were, I doubt very much that Unity Movement members, either collectively or individually, read Heidegger.

However, had they done so, Unity Movement adherents would have found in the pages of *Was Heißt Denken?* a fellow traveler. To be so aligned with Heidegger would, I suspect, have provided them no solace and succor at all; indeed, it might have offended them—that is, if it did not out-rage them. However, their slogan "Education Before Liberation," a po-litical strategy completely at odds with the populism of the African National Congress (ANC), reveals the foundation of their class con-sciousness and is also of a piece—an uncomfortable piece, but of a piece nonetheless—with Heidegger's refusal of the notion that human beings "think too much and act too little."[18] It is, rather, that we "act too much and think too little."[19] With its deep commitment to education, its sus-picion of action for its own sake, and its principled opposition to popu-lism, the Unity Movement enjoined disenfranchised South Africans to be cautious of injunctions to act without thinking or act before having thought. Heidegger and the Unity Movement are strange bedfellows; because both are intellectuals to a fault.

The slogan "Education Before Liberation"[20] was more often, at least by my generation, transformed from a strict telos into a simultaneity. In fact, my generation conjoined these two ostensibly opposing injunctions into mutually transforming and supporting parts, resolving the dialec-tic, insofar as such a resolution is possible. We conjoined them into a new slogan: "Liberation Through Education." In Heidegger's terms, this means acting and thinking in equal measure. To their credit, Livingstone teachers—and all others of their ilk—not only supported us as students during the 1976 and 1980 school boycotts, they also engaged us. What is more, they made us account for our decision to stop attending classes and demanded that we provide an alternative structure for our school day. They also distinguished themselves by assisting us with political pro-gramming and provided, when needed (and sometimes even when they were not asked), political advice.

Heidegger and the Unity Movement intelligentsia were both crea-tures of the Book.

All dedicated to the primacy of the mind (the Unity Movement was a soirée culture—think red wine, books, discussion groups, high-brow music) and promoted the mind as the first and most enduring political weapon.

It is no wonder, then, that Unity Movement members steeped them-selves in what they considered the Classics. Epigrammatically conceived, the Classics encompass that canon of literature that runs, broadly speaking, from the Greeks to Chaucer, Shakespeare, and the Romantics; from Marx, Trotsky, Lenin, and Rosa Luxembourg to James. As such, the canon defined the intellectual horizon for the disenfranchised middle classes, at least in the political environ that was the greater Cape Town area (what constitutes, in local geography, the Western Cape region of South Africa).

For this class, the popular would forever bear the mark of *vulgus*—strictly for the common people, for the riffraff.

This was not so for R. O. For all his erudition and the "Classical" makeup of his library, Mr. Dudley was no snob. The popular, in its many iterations—from his interest in the programming on offer from the newly established South African Broadcasting Corporation, to sport (he sometimes umpired interhouse school cricket matches), to his bemused (but not always benign) view of new cultural trends (ear-ringed teenage boys were an object of fascination and mildly ironic scorn to him)—was a series of practices worthy of study to Mr. Dudley.

As such, if my claim about R. O.'s popular, cultural studies–inflected sensibility (Hall and Paddy Whannel studied the emerging popular cinema, popular music, and working-class reading practices in *The Popular Arts*[21]) has any merit, then I am free to speculate about the expanse of his popular taste. Did R. O. watch *Dallas*, a soap opera that was by far the most watched television show not only in the United States and South Africa but in many other sites across the globe? (In the 1950s, when soap operas first debuted on U.S. television, James, as we know, watched them obsessively during his stay in this country.) If R. O. did, and I fervently hope he did, then I am sure he would have produced more than a critique of that strange political animal, the U.S. class system. Possessed as R. O. was of a mischievous bent, I wonder what he made of all those Ewing family machinations (sex, infidelity, the desire for power, and so on) and all that oil-derived economic intrigue, which always turned on the underhanded schemes concocted by J. R., the oldest son and the show's pantomime villain. Who, in R. O.'s estimation, was responsible for shooting J. R.? That is the surest test of Mr. Dudley's popular credentials (that is, as long as we acknowledge that everything in R. O. mitigated against populism). That was the biggest cliff-hanger in popular culture and a question that consumed even the most lukewarm *Dallas* fan.

Impeccable as R. O.'s anti-apartheid political credentials were—he had, after all, served time on political charges—and as unmatched as he was pedagogically, it is, in retrospect, his ability to think in different registers, one seemingly unrelated to the other, that I did not grasp at all. I should have known better.

"Permanent Revolution"

R. O.'s view of the world was shaped above all by the work of Leon Trotsky. There was almost no way we could have been aware of it, at least not then. In our Livingstone days, we could have sensed it only dimly, and even that I strongly doubt. However, Livingstone was a world made in the image of Trotsky's *Permanent Revolution*.[22] What R. O. sought to instill in us was less an absolute familiarity with the text itself—although he would have approved of such an undertaking—than a fidelity to Trotsky's concept of the need to infinitely renew the revolution. The work of history is to always be ready to do the work of infinite renewal and rededication. In Derrida's energy-sapping rendering, the work of politics is to begin again, as if for the first time. (Consider also the unexpectedly dialectical terms of the motto of the Netflix series *Stranger Things*: "Every ending has a beginning.") As Jameson plainly notes, "History is what hurts."[23] The catastrophe—corruption emanating from the very highest levels of government, massive inequity, degradation of the environment, and widespread hopelessness, to mention but a few—that is postapartheid South Africa finds a bathos-filled resonance in Jameson's definition of *history* as that form of political experience that "refuses desire and sets inexorable limits to individual as well as collective praxis, which its 'ruses' turn into grisly and ironic reversals of their overt intention."[24] R. O.'s vision of a postapartheid society has certainly turned into a grisly and ironic reversal of his overt intention. The ironies of history are cruel—so cruel, we might say, as to make of Trotsky's call for permanent revolution a fundamental political virtue. This is appropriate, of course, given the painful lessons—the early optimism notwithstanding—that Trotsky recounts in his *History of the Russian Revolution* and is compelled to think again in *The Revolution Betrayed*.

The Livingstone Milieu

If it is R. O. who embodied G.W.F. Hegel's "World Historical Idea" and his "Spirit" too (making him the closest thing Livingstone had to its own homegrown "World Historical Figure"), then he was surrounded by "thinking men [*sic*], who had insight into the requirements of the time— *what was ripe for development*. This was the very Truth for their age, for their world."[25] Livingstone was a high school saturated with radical ideas, beginning with a profound opposition to apartheid. Nonetheless, our teachers followed, sometimes more scrupulously than others, the CAD syllabus, preparing their students for the national exams they would take at the end of their matriculation year. Our teachers refused, however, to miseducate a single Livingstone student.

To this end, R. O. gathered around him a group of teachers dedicated to making the Livingstone student body think.

Disenfranchised as we were under apartheid, at Livingstone we were educated by intellectuals. Those of us who attended institutions such as Livingstone[26] *were instructed by teachers*[27] *who, whether they would have acceded to such a description of their pedagogical endeavors or not, were given to thinking—and thinking deeply.*

There, in those Livingstone classrooms, a range of subjects—English, Afrikaans, physics, biology, mathematics, German, geography, history, accounting, art, and woodwork among them—were taught by teachers who instructed their students into thinking. United as they were in their opposition to apartheid, our teachers—almost every single one of them a committed instructor—instilled in us, their charges, above all else, a desire for thinking.

There were no readers of Heidegger among them—of that, I am sure. But it was thinking they taught us before anything else.

My English teachers, the premier one whom we meet in the next chapter, were exceptional. Peter Fiske taught all manner of poetry, ranging from the Romantics to the Modernists. He also exhibited outstanding taste in music. Mr. Fiske introduced me to one Robert Allen Zimmerman. I came to Bob Dylan as a fourteen-year-old student courtesy of Mr. Fiske.

After hearing Mr. Fiske play a Dylan song in class for us to analyze (how freaking cool was that? This was in 1977, the heyday of disco), I went out and bought my first—and then Dylan's most recent—LP, his 1978 *Street Legal*. I still have it. (Even though disco was ascendant, Mr. Fiske remained, in spirit and self-presentation, with his flowing beard, hair a little unkempt, a child of the '60s. Dylan would have been just Mr. Fiske's speed then. What is more, Dylan would win a Nobel for his poetry in 2016,[28] so Peter Fiske was almost forty years ahead of the game.) *Street Legal* has traveled with me from Cape Town, to New York City, to Detroit, Michigan, to western Massachusetts, to Durham, North Carolina, before coming to a well-earned, extended rest in my home in Ithaca, New York. On the cover of *Street Legal*, there's Dylan, all louche.

This was just before Dylan went—who'd a thunk it?—Christian fundamentalist. Around 1979, Dylan, the Jewish kid from the hardscrabble Midwest, became an evangelical Christian, putting out three albums—*Slow Train Coming* (1979), *Saved* (1979), and *Shot of Love* (1981)—documenting this most unlikely of spiritual dalliances. ("Everybody's gotta serve somebody.")[29] By 1982, Dylan's flirtation with Christianity was over, and he returned to something like his counterculture self with an LP entitled, appropriately, *Infidels*.

In November 2019, more than forty years after first encountering him, I saw him live in concert for the third time. If anything, his diction was worse, but his aura remains undiminished.

"Do you love me or are you just extending good will?"[30] were the lines I sang in my head as I read the faded plaque commemorating Dylan's birth in rundown Duluth, Minnesota, in the summer of 2020. (Dylan was raised in Hibbing, but his mother gave birth to him at a Catholic hospital in Duluth.) We've come a long way together, Bobby D. and I. At least, that's how I see things as I take in Dylan's recent *Rough and Rowdy Ways* (2020; his thirty-ninth studio album). On *Rough and Rowdy Ways*, his music and distinctive voice, raspier and less intelligible than I remember it just three years ago, put one ever more in mind of a bluesman such as Buddy Guy.

During our winter and spring breaks, Mr. Fiske led us on hikes in the Cedarberg mountains, some four hours north of Cape Town near the town of Clanwilliam, where the earth runs red and citrus farms—with their orchards of oranges, lemons, and tangerines—abound. The last important thing I did before leaving South Africa for the United States in 1989 was to climb the Cedarberg one last time with my oldest friend, B., with whom I'd made that first trek up the mountain in September 1977. B. and I led a party on the same path—from the Welberdacht cave, where we always camp on the first night, up to the Wolfberg Arch, then back to the forester's station—that we had first hiked under Mr. Fiske's guidance.

Lawrence DuPlooy was our class (homeroom) teacher in 1977. Dupie,[31] as he was known then and continues to be known, also taught us physical science in 1977 and would do so until we graduated in 1980. (Mrs. MacArthur served as our class teacher in 1978 and 1979.) Himself a Livingstone alum (class of 1968), Mr. DuPlooy, an engineering student who found himself sidetracked into teaching, struck me then as a young man possessed of a certain joie de vivre and puckishness. He was quick with a joke but rigorous in his pedagogy.[32] I remain in contact with him (as I did briefly with Mr. Fiske), as do many of my classmates. A popular figure at Livingstone, he quit teaching in 1982, but despite all the years that have passed, I can rely on Mr. DuPlooy, now retired from his engineering career, to keep me abreast of developments as they pertain to the class of 1980.

In sharp contrast to Mr. DuPlooy was *Meneer* (Mister) Van Zyl. Standing well over six feet and of considerable heft to boot (he filled out his jacket and trousers), Meneer Van Zyl—the honorific seemed pro forma, so imposing a figure was he—taught my class Afrikaans in our two final years. He oozed authority. I have been moved to speculate that this sense of his authority could be accounted for in part by his propensity for grammatical singularity. In his native tongue, Meneer Van Zyl eschewed simple temporal formulation. The simple past or present tense was, gathering from his aversion to using it, beneath him. The simple declarative present tense, it would seem, presented no challenge. It might indeed have made his speech, well, ordinary.

And Meneer Van Zyl was no *gewone* (ordinary) Afrikaner.

It was widely known that, unlike many of his kinfolk, he did not support the apartheid regime's politics. And, much as he towered over everyone, his demeanor was that of a rigid politeness.

Distinct about Meneer Van Zyl was that he always addressed us in the present continuous tense, a grammatical peculiarity that derived from his abiding attachment to the imperative. Our class was a rowdy bunch, especially after returning from our interval (the equivalent of a lunch break in an American school). If we had him for Afrikaans, he never asked us to be quiet—"*Stilte asseblief*" ("Please be quiet").

He never said it that way; it was always this distinct grammatical construction: "*Daar word nou stil gebly*" ("There will now be silence"). This he pronounced as from on high, as if he were an Old Testament prophet come to Livingstone life, commanding us into a future that was not yet but would arrive soon. Even the most boisterous among us fell into a dutiful silence. Such was the effect of Meneer van Zyl's use of the future imperative tense.

Even now, more than four decades after I last passed through the decorated arch that marks the school's opening as a student, I can only recall—nay, understand—"Fannie" (pronounced FAH-Nee), the students' nickname for him, as the very embodiment of the declarative.

In a conversation with Mr. DuPlooy in June 2021, I inquired after Meneer Van Zyl, only to be told that he had passed on.

Daar word nou stil gebly. There will now be silence. A moment of silence must now be marked for a remarkable teacher.

And yet I can recall Fannie and his considerable presence with ease. There he is, a man who loved polyester outfits (it was the '70s, what can I say?), filling the entryway to our classroom, clad in a checked jacket with a matching pair of green pants, a horizontally striped shirt, a broad tie, as befits the era, with bold vertical stripes, a boldness that managed to never cross over into garishness.

There will now be sadness out of regard for a remarkable teacher.

I was not, however, enamored of all my teachers. I'd have swapped my biology and mathematics teachers of my two final years at Livingstone for a mess of pottage. They'd have agreed to the swap without hesitation; there was no love lost there, on either side.

I recall them with no fondness and miss them not at all.

Come to think of it, I could say the same about my standard 8 biology teacher.

Clearly, there is something about me and biology teachers.

In Gratitude

When I was a high school student, this was my anti-apartheid apartheid education, and I cannot help but express gratitude for the Livingstone education I received. I express gratitude to this very day. Of course, by expressing gratitude to and for my Livingstone education, I am, whether I want to or not, whether I seek to escape the dialectic or not, making an equivalent gesture in the direction of the apartheid state. Specifically, I am expressing gratitude for my apartheid education.

The pedagogical gift that emerged out of my CAD experience is that I was instructed by my teachers, beginning with R. O. but by no means limited to him, to think. These teachers demanded that their Livingstone pupils think, regardless of the conditions in which we found ourselves. A CAD education could inhibit but never prohibit the singular demand to think. If an institution such as Livingstone made any history under apartheid, it can be distilled to a single recognition. The only way to live under the conditions that was a CAD education was through a constitutively—constituently—dialectical relationship with apartheid education. This meant it was necessary to apprehend apartheid's strictures as ground zero for thinking. Thinking begins in and with—and against and despite—an apartheid education.

Apartheid could not know how its effects would locate thinking at the core of its educational inequity. This is the truth of the event: Its effects, the forces it will unleash in the world, the pathways it will open up, the restrictions it will impose, and the possibilities it will enable or foreclose are known only to it. The event is true to itself and only itself.

And so, in the ethical framework that is the event—like it or not, aware of it or not—apartheid (itself) was ripe for nothing so much as thinking.

There was, as my Livingstone experience attests, nothing to do but think, nothing to do but think apartheid. What a gift apartheid bestowed upon us.

And, like every gift, the event must have a name. In this instance, one name stands above all: Richard Owen Dudley—a symptomatic name, an asymptomatic name, now one, now the other.

Richard Owen Dudley was an exceptional teacher; the exception, as well know, is what proves the rule. In Mr. Dudley's case, however, the force of the exception depends only marginally on its difference from the norm, which is what affords the exception its exemplarity.

In Richard Owen Dudley's case, the logic of the exception turns on a singular metric. R. O. was exceptional because he was able to distinguish himself by virtue of sheer stamina. His intensity, in our Deleuze- and Félix Guattari-derived understanding of the concept, never slackened. In every encounter, with every student, the intensity of being toward thinking was palpable.

To be in R. O.'s presence was to know the effect of a mind constantly at odds with the maleficent designs of a CAD education. Because of him, apartheid's "regime of veridiction"[33] found itself opposed and disrupted daily, confronted by a set of propositions that did not rely on a set of apartheid rules for their sustainability. As Michel Foucault explains it, the effect of a regime of veridiction is not to determine whether a statement is true or false; rather, it is to ask under what conditions things—in this case the miseducation of successive generations of disenfranchised students—can be or can be made possible. A regime of veridiction is not, as we might be tempted to assume, truth or a set of truths. *Veritas*, after all, is the Latin noun for "truth." Instead, a regime of veridiction is the establishment of a set of rules that determines which statements can be considered true and which false. (In this regard, Theodor Adorno is much more direct: The "truth of logic is its coercive character."[34] The logic of apartheid was nothing if not coercive, both in its character and in its practice.) A discursive regime, in other words, is tailor-made for the rhetorical and ideological project that was apartheid; it is that regime through which apartheid racism could "veridict" itself. Apartheid established itself as a set of truths through which, say, CAD or IAD education could offer (this education as) justifications for the racial oppression imposed on South Africa's disenfranchised. (Foucault presented these lectures on biopolitics from late 1978 to the spring of 1979, at which moment the Livingstone class of 1980, entering standard 9, began to turn its attention to life after matriculation.)

In setting himself against apartheid's regime of veridiction and instructing us into his practice, R. O. returned the distinction between true and false into a difference of historical import.

R. O. would rather, I am sure, have had his charges succumb to the lure of the *pensée sauvage* (the "savage mind") than to docilely submit to the dictates of a CAD syllabus.

Fortunately for Livingstone students, that choice was never presented.

Instead, R. O. embodied, literally, an intensity of the mind—an intensity his avuncularity and appetite for mischief (he was quick with a joke and possessed of a sometimes droll but almost always wicked sense of humor) did nothing to disguise.

An R. O. Joke

R. O. was well known—and fondly remembered in some quarters, both at Livingstone and far beyond—for his atheism. In February 1980, when R. O. was acting principal (the principal, Mr. Evans, was on sabbatical), a minor fundamentalist brouhaha broke out at the school. A man of science—but more importantly, a man who located himself within the trajectory of the Enlightenment—R. O. was well shot of any form of organized religion. When the minor fundamentalist clamor reached its peak, R. O., ever the creature of Reason, intoned with quiet authority but with just a hint of smile at the corners of his mouth: "I will take on the Pope and the Ayatollah on two conditions: that they are both sane and sober." The pope, by R. O.'s reckoning, would be eliminated on the grounds of sobriety; for his part, the ayatollah would be disqualified on the grounds of sanity.

In late 2022, R. O. would, I am sure, be on the side of those Iranians, especially the women, protesting the suppression of the current theocratic regime, where chants of "Death to the Dictator" are now a daily utterance, buttressed as it is by the rallying cry "Women, Life, Liberty" (an event set in motion by the September 16, 2022, death of Mahsa Amini at the hands of Iran's morality police). With the calls for a secular democracy issuing from every sector of Iranian society and across the spectrum of ethnic communities, R. O. might have concluded that the desire for modernity cannot be stayed.

He might have saluted the bravery of the Iranian protesters and raised a glass to them. In return, it is likely that many an Iranian, from all walks of life, would have raised a glass of aragh—a traditional Iranian vodka to him.[35]

Today, what with *il papa*'s well-known affection for Scotch that is complicated by Francis's populism (most often rendered as his riding the bus to work during his tenure as archbishop of Buenos Aires), R. O. would find himself in a slight conundrum, one he might again (although in a more leisurely spirit) resolve over a glass of fine red wine.

As for the state capture by Iran's Revolutionary Guard, R. O. would surely have a field day with that.[36]

Darstellung, The Final Word

From his Enlightenment humor to his cultural studies acumen, R. O. commanded his intensity, marshaling it always in the cause of thinking. In this regard, his exceptionality is singular. The effect of his intensity was its ability to radiate outward. Moving through a series of concentric circles, it radiated from Mr. Dudley to his colleagues, and then from the faculty to the students. A milieu of intensity was born at 100 Lansdowne Road, dispersed across the entirety of the institution, nurtured, and maintained, creating out of its dispersal what Jean-Paul Sartre names a "synthetic universality."[37] This occurred as if through osmosis, as befits a man of science, but it was always a process with an identifiable core, a process that emanated from a rare centrifugal force: R. O., a figure on the order of Sartre's "singular universal," the name Sartre gives to the intellectual, and not always affirmatively, such as it is presented here. For Sartre, the work of the intellectual is to "discover his own contradiction."[38] There is an unrelenting contestation between the universal and the particular, producing in the intellectual an "unhappy consciousness."[39] Out of the ferment that is an unhappy consciousness, the radical Sartrean intellectual is born. The singular, if at all possible, can only be overcome by the intellectual—who is, for Sartre, predominantly bourgeois (and male)—who "ceaselessly combats his own class" and understands that the universal "perpetually remains to be achieved."[40] The intellectual has to guard against the temptations of his class (which Sartrean history urges him to betray) but also has to be wary of nationalism, racism, and imperialism, as the universal could so easily become chauvinistic.

What Sartre takes to be the intellectual's limited capacity for self-awareness resonates differently in regard to R. O. According to Sartre, the "intellectual's thought must ceaselessly turn back on itself in order always to apprehend itself as a *singular universal*."[41] The rigor of self-reflection entails the absolute need to think the self in its class location. (Saliently, Sartre's pessimism here about the intellectual's aptitude for self-consciousness turns almost immediately to a critique of racism, which he designates the "ideology of imperialism," and of, in short, the indelibility of racism, of racism as an ineradicable force.)[42]

If R. O. was, as has been suggested, the incarnation of institutional memory, if he was the keeper of the Livingstone flame, then this was a role he accepted in the spirit of Socrates. The institution as the purveyor of value (ideas, ideology, a mode of being in apartheid society), in R. O.'s fidelity to it, could only endure if it was made a subject for thinking. ("All history is bunk," as Henry Ford so famously proclaimed. It is bunk if history is not subjected to interrogation. We return to this Ford insight in the Stan Ridge chapter.) R. O. was relentless in his questioning of the institution, beginning with his role in it. He asked questions of himself ceaselessly. He knew what his standing in the community was, and because of this, he understood the importance of self-awareness.

As the "singular universal," he stood as the embodiment of all that is possible—an embodiment that began from the basis of philosophical first principles: Know thyself.

R. O. knew what he bore; he understood that the possibilities for a different mode of being under apartheid were contained within him, a single teacher, the singular, exceptional teacher, that teacher in tension not only with his own class but with all other social formations seeking to achieve hegemony. In a word, Mr. Dudley was possessed of a Sartrean intellectual style. For him, being an intellectual was "no more than a means of presenting being-in-the-world."[43] It was a mode of "being-in-the-world" that all around R. O. sought, to some degree or other, to emulate. Such was the force, reductively phrased, of Mr. Dudley's "singular universality."[44]

His intensity, then, rather than being reduced in its effects as it radiated from the core, gathered new force each time a new concentric circle was formed, much like a storm. The intensity intensified, sometimes proceeding in an ordered, predictable fashion, other times threatening chaos, disrupting everything in its immediate vicinity and reaching well beyond it.

This is the kind of intensity that students at Livingstone experienced in 1976 with the Soweto school riots, which quickly found their way to 100 Lansdowne Road, and again in 1980, when high schools in the Western Cape became the focal point of anti-apartheid resistance.

What should be evident to us now, even if it escaped us those several decades ago, is that Richard Owen Dudley's *Darstellung* (which no one has ever mistaken for dissembling) bears testimony to the many registers in which his intensity articulated itself. (From Kant to Hegel to Louis Althusser and beyond, *Darstellung* has a complex history. Above all, however, it is a critique of the Enlightenment notion of representation where there is the presumption of a direct correspondence between subject and object. The invocation of the term here signals how it is we struggle to grasp the world but, more importantly in relation to R. O., how it is the general is experienced by an individual such as R. O. in a distinct and singular way. As we will see later, Althusser, in reading the term through Marx, will arrive at a distinctly economistic derivation of the term.)[45] Inclining toward thinking is the first and most enduring of those intensities. This intensity is constituted out of the propensity for living in tension, for embracing the difficulty that ordained thought to "progress by contradiction" and, as such, to live in an "antagonistic unity" with the self.[46]

In short, the gift of the dialectic as the demand for thinking how to be in the world. Out of perversity comes gratitude; out of the most adverse conditions for pedagogy emerges a lifelong commitment to thinking.

To be trained to think while knowing, and then only dimly (if even that), that the self is being taught to think.

Interlude I

Education for Barbarism

Isaac Bangani Tabata (better known as I. B. or Tabby), a Trotskyist and one of the founders of the Non-European Unity Movement, wrote the pamphlet *Education for Barbarism* in 1956. In its content, Tabata's title served as a stinging and resonant political critique of BAD. It also provided anti-apartheid forces with a handy slogan with which to attack the apartheid regime's policy of "separate education."[1] CAD and BAD were, of course, the pedagogical corollary to, among other policies, the apartheid government's separate living areas (known as the Group Areas Act), its separate sports facilities, and its criminalization of marriage across apartheid's racial categories (known as the Mixed Marriages Act). There was also the Immorality Act, which forbade sexual relations between South Africans of different races. Tabata's indictment guided Livingstone teachers in their pedagogical approach.

More importantly, however, his critique did not relieve anti-CAD teachers of their responsibility to their charges in the classroom.

CAD and IAD education had to be ideologically understood—that is, Tabata sought to make evident the intended deleteriousness of CAD education. For all that, however, CAD was the only educational game in town, and disenfranchised students remained to be educated, no matter the barbarous intentions of the apartheid regime and its CAD syllabus.

A Brief Excursus: Deleuze and Guattari

Before we return to Tabata, a quick detour through Deleuze and Guattari is necessary, in part because of the amplification they offer Tabata's critique and in equal measure because of how their thinking deepens our understanding of what Tabata might have to offer. According to Deleuze and Guattari, philosophy has only one task: To create concepts. That is their answer to the titular question they pose in their work *What Is Philosophy?* Every concept, they assert, has a "signature"—"Descartes's cogito, Liebniz's nomad, Kant's condition," and so on.[2] However, "some concepts must be indicated by an extraordinary and sometimes even barbarous or shocking word."[3] In non-accordance with Tabata, we might say, the concept that is the perversity of gratitude can only be brought into thinking through the barbarous and shocking provocation on which the concept turns—depends, we can go so far as to insist. The question becomes *What can that which is deemed barbarous and shocking bring to light that nothing else can?* The answer is remarkably self-evident: The perversity of gratitude reveals, through deliberate explication and careful extrication (retrieval from and even the "shocking" appropriation of), how a disenfranchised education created the conditions for the disenfranchised to think.

The perversity of gratitude is that concept that demands a philosophical confrontation in and through the very act of creating—*creating* is the key, rather Foucauldian term upon which Deleuze and Guattari insist—the concept. While Deleuze and Guattari are clear that the "decisive definition" of philosophy is "knowledge through pure concepts," in the case of the perversity of gratitude, that which they hold to be secondary and less efficacious might actually provide a keener insight into what it is the perversity of gratitude makes possible.[4] Deleuze and Guattari write:

> To know oneself, to learn to think, to act as if nothing were self-evident—wondering, "wondering that there is being"—these, and many other determinations of philosophy create interesting attitudes, however tiresome they may be in the long run, but even from

a pedagogical point of view they do not constitute a well-defined occupation or precise activity.[5]

The critique here of Heidegger—"'wondering that there is being'"—is impossible to miss, especially because Deleuze and Guattari seem to ride roughshod over the very precision that is Heidegger's trademark in this regard. The question of Being is *the* question to which Heidegger's oeuvre is entirely felicitous. The existence of Being is not in question, and it is certainly not a question with which Heidegger exercises himself for any significant length of time. (Delueuze and Guattari's critique is intensified when they minimize the "pedagogical point of view," because, as we know, Heidegger was nothing if not first a teacher. We could say the same about Foucault, as his many published lectures make evident.)

However, in the spirit of non-accordance, what Deleuze and Guattari make possible is the bringing into concordance of the concept and the opportunity to "know oneself, to learn to think, to act as if nothing were self-evident." In so doing, what emerges is the substantiation of the concept. Instead of standing in a difficult and an oppositional relationship to each other, the concept and the praxes Deleuze and Guattari are somewhat impatient with actually serve each other well in this context. The concept that is the perversity of gratitude is one that goes counter to the received wisdom of CAD education; "learning to think" in the terms that the concept sets forth is precisely to act without what we might term "foreknowledge." The concept is the provocation to thinking, and as such, it undertakes to guarantee nothing. Its only guarantee is that it offers no guarantees.

The concept is in this way akin to a felicitous use of the archive. While it may have some notion of the kind of critique it would like to produce and may presume an architecture and a mode of construction, the perversity of gratitude is never sure of what it will unearth, what it will render, what will emerge out of or because of it. The archive, in these terms, can then be said to be functioning as it should. The archive is true to itself because the archive is that mode of engagement—research, let us name it, without any great confidence—with a body of work that does nothing so much as surprise. What you find in the archive is not at all what you expected to find in the archive. The archive, in the best possible sense, leads you astray. (It is likely to, as Žižek might have it, "short circuit" us in our work. It brings to light that which is "unthought," Žižek's invocation of a Heideggerian principle.)[6] The perversity of gratitude offers no assurances and makes of its transgressions the pathway to a series of unexpected insights. New knowledge can emerge, as opposed to, if such a poor phrasing might be indulged, "knew knowledge"—"knowledge" that was already "known" in advance of the encounter with the archive.

As such, there is nothing to do but agree with Deleuze and Guattari. Thinking the concept, thinking in the terms of the perversity of gratitude, confronting the difficulties that the concept presents, that in fact constitute the core of the concept, will not make of this undertaking a "well-defined occupation." Thinking, as Heidegger so often reminds us, is by no means a "precise activity." Instead, the concept is premised on the very condition that "nothing is self-evident." Indeed, as has already been established, were we to proceed from that which is presumed to be "self-evident," we would already have concluded that BAD, CAD, and IAD education was a barbarous assault on the disenfranchised mind. That, after all, is the perceived wisdom against which *The Perversity of Gratitude* has taken its stand.

It is for this reason that to think is to begin from the premise that the very notion of "received wisdom" is at best a question and at worst a mode of apprehension entirely incompatible with any serious form of philosophical inquiry.

By not submitting to the logic of opposites, non-accordance recognizes in Deleuze and Guattari an edification of the concept through attending to the practices that derive from it and, in so doing, strengthening the concept. Deleuze and Guattari offer us something in this regard when they discuss the concept in relation to Nietzsche. They write, "According to the Nietzschean verdict, you will know nothing through concepts unless you have first created them."[7] In creating concepts, we come to know them. In creating them, we come to know what lines of flight—that most Deleuzian of concepts—might be pursued. What is more, the concept makes it possible to follow lines of flight that we could not have anticipated when first bringing the concept into being.

In Barbarism, A Philosophical Promise

Out of the ideological conflict to which Tabata gave discursive form (and an adjectival phrasing), out of this pedagogical foment, with Tabata's critique reverberating in several timbres simultaneously, it became possible—necessary, even, it seems to me—to think. What Tabata feared and sought to forestall—that the disenfranchised would be made intellectually unfit for life in the modern world—could, paradoxically, only be achieved by not only opposing apartheid but by doing so dialectically and thinking against apartheid from within the interstices that CAD, per force, gave life to. The inclining to thinking was the creation not of ideological intent but the consequence of being instructed by teachers wise to the workings of the dialectic, even if they were not practicing Trotskyists, Marxists, or Leninists. What Tabata's concept reveals is that the dialectic is the inevitable outcome of *knowing*,[8] as a sentient disenfranchised being, apartheid. Such a knowing, which is by no means a mere knowing, was enough, in and of itself, to make of the dialectic a lived reality within the CAD classroom.

The dialectical effect of Tabata's critique was to impose on teachers of the disenfranchised a singular responsibility. In order to educate the disenfranchised for something more than barbarism, there could be no diminution of pedagogical expectation, beginning with the demand placed on Livingstone teachers that they dedicate themselves to one cause above all others: Intellectual rigor. In R. O. Dudley, Livingstone had just such a teacher, one who stood explicitly against any classroom endeavor that countenanced a disenfranchised education that laid any of its students open to the charge of barbarism. Such a pedagogical outcome would have been intolerable to R. O.

It is now clearer to me than ever. Five years of Livingstone education sought to begin a process that would, over the course of a lifetime, produce beings who would, as a matter of philosophical course, think their place in the world. Until 1990, when the apartheid regime effectively relinquished power, Livingstone trained its students to think their place in the world. Students were taught to think for themselves a mode of being in the world other than that perpetual disenfranchisement to which apartheid was determined to condemn them. (Tabata died at eighty-one in October 1990 in exile in Harare, Zimbabwe. Tabata died a short eight months after Nelson Mandela was released from prison and the black liberation movements were unbanned by the apartheid regime.) Ironically enough, Tabata and the apartheid regime subscribed, no matter their diametrically opposed positions, to the same horizon of expectation. Both Tabata and the regime expected that disenfranchised students would emerge out of CAD as the barbarous offspring of an ideologically malignant pedagogy. Caliban-like, it was the anticipation of both opposing forces that we CAD students would have been miseducated to a monstrous degree, our capacity for thinking undone by that which was intended to do eternal violence to disenfranchised minds. Caliban, we remember, revolted against the very language Prospero gave him: "The red plague rid you for learning me your language."[9] Caliban, of course, rages against Prospero in the very language that Prospero gave him. Our Livingstone teachers instilled in us the desire to secure a language that could bear the weight of thinking. That was the language that we were, in and through our dialectical struggle with/against apartheid, crafting for ourselves. This language was not a Calibanesque plague, then; it was, it turns out, a Heideggerian gift.

Concepts 2

As Saint Augustine in his fine *Confessions,*
Which make the reader envy his transgressions.

—**Lord Byron,** *Don Juan*

Transgression

A perversity striated, in the (tormented) spirit of Augustine, with the markings—rude streaks—of transgression. For Augustine, perversity stands as the act of willful transgression against God, the "thrill of acting against Your Law."[1] Augustine's is a spirit that infuses *The Perversity of Gratitude*, although there is almost nothing of the tormented (believer) about this writing. Augustine famously committed his willful transgression, stealing a neighbor's pears, at the age of sixteen ("deed wrought in that dark night when I was sixteen"[2]). For its part, *The Perversity of Gratitude* is a decades-long reflection on eighteen years of apartheid education (high school, college—"university" in South African parlance). While this writing is free of Augustine's self-loathing ("For I had any number of better pears of my own, and plucked only those that I might steal")[3] and self-recrimination ("For once I had gathered them I threw them away, tasting only my own sin and savouring that with delight,")[4] it is a writing born out of the ongoing struggle—a struggle that has its origins deep in the self—over the determination to so perversely attribute gratitude to an apartheid education.[5] In this regard, however, Augustine might be understood as the figure through which a modicum of re-demption is achieved. *The Perversity of Gratitude* appropriates Au-gustine's profound regret at his youthful appetite for willful trans-gression and renders transgression as that disruptive intellectual force that must be *thought* out of perversity and can only be thought because of perversity.

A series of transgressive acts, a modulation of transgression, a transgression that operates in many registers: Some of these regis-ters are bold and affirming, others hesitant and less certain of them-selves, and still others so subtle as to be difficult to identify. It is the time and place of his transgression that so haunt Augustine. It is time and place that make of his adolescent transgression an event that must be written. So, here, too, is writing overdetermined by place, that place I am tempted to name as the scene, the spectral site, of a perverse crime.

There Is No Such Thing as a Constitutive Outside

Apartheid is a primal scene in the history of thinking. It is a primal scene out of which an unarguable recognition emerges. There is no such thing as a constitutive outside. Apartheid enveloped every-thing within it. It touched on every aspect of life—for the disenfran-chised as well as for the ruling white minority. Apartheid imposed itself on everything.

Everything began with apartheid. There was no end to it.

Apartheid constituted life and, because of its omnipresence, it had to be confronted. Because it denied the possibility of a consti-tutive outside, apartheid demanded that it be thought. That which will not allow us to be outside of it, to live in relief from it, leaves us without a choice.

If apartheid is everything and everything derives from apartheid, then apartheid, in all its effects, must be made the first—and some-times the only—subject for thinking.

Again, we find ourselves face-to-face with perversity. That which works determinedly against thinking, because of its omnipresence and, indeed, its omnipotence, presents itself so relentlessly in every facet of life as that which must be thought.

To know that there is no constitutive outside is to know that the experience of apartheid in general—and an apartheid education in particular—marks the self indelibly.

Whether one is within the regime of apartheid or removed physically from its environs matters not. Apartheid is that experience that cannot be escaped. It remains lodged within the self permanently, despite the fact that formal apartheid has ended or that the disenfranchised self no longer resides physically within the confines of postapartheid South Africa.

The perversity of a disenfranchised apartheid education is that this education must, a priori, be thought in terms of the many ways in which apartheid has formed the disenfranchised self's understanding of itself. To know that there is no constitutive outside is to acknowledge that the disenfranchised self must know that it began to know itself from within the logic of apartheid. This logic is so antagonistic to that formation of self because it is a logic committed to the racist, discriminatory, systemic inequality of the disenfranchised self. The disenfranchised self must know that every question about itself begins from within a logic of apartheid designed to circumscribe the life—the horizon of and for thinking—of the disenfranchised self and to destroy the disenfranchised self as a matter of course. Apartheid as utterly indifferent to the fate of the individual disenfranchised self.

The disenfranchised self must know that its being in the world is unthinkable outside of apartheid.

The disenfranchised self owes itself to apartheid.

What could be more perverse than that?

This is what it means to live the condition of knowing that there is no possibility of being (as a disenfranchised being) outside of apartheid.

What could be more perverse than that?

There is no constitution of (a disenfranchised) self outside of the very forces that are so violent and antipathetic to the constitution of that self.

The perversity of gratitude articulates the disenfranchised self's indebtedness to apartheid. An unpayable debt emerges out of a profound injury to the self that is—was—incurred. It is an injury for which there can be no restitution. The thinking indebted to the perversity of gratitude is the only viable form of reparation that can be offered, that was long since offered, to the disenfranchised self.

Perverse.

II

Morgan MacArthur

English Teacher Nonpareil

The unobtrusive intellectual operates, with great effectiveness, in the lower registers—or, in Ralph Ellison's terms, "on the lower frequencies."[1] The most unobtrusively intellectual of my teachers instructed me in English.

In our first years of high school, standards 6 and 7, our English teachers at Livingstone were charged with instructing us in the finer points of English grammar and literature. The approved syllabus for CAD students consisted of identifying parts of speech and becoming adept in the close reading of a poem, skills we would later put to good use as we graduated to literature—novels and drama—which we were first introduced to in standard 7.

Close reading imparted real analytical skills. However, had the CAD syllabus taken its pedagogical cue directly from the *Scrutiny* project of F. R. and Queenie Leavis, it might have imparted an altogether more valuable set of insights. *Scrutiny*, after all, sought to establish a critical foundation—a set of praxes for reading—for this new discipline named "English." (This discipline signaled a break with the Classical education that held sway in Oxbridge colleges, where the study of Classical languages and cultures and Greek and Latin dominated. It was a discipline born out of the instrumentalist need of the British Empire to educate colonial officials into their own culture, of which British literature was a crucial component. Chaucer, Shakespeare, and Byron could only be effectively taught to the colonized if the colonial administrators themselves had more than a passing familiarity with it. This is also true for the history that was the Battle of Hastings, William the Conqueror, the Bill of Rights, the Magna Carta, and the machinations of Cromwell's Republican revolution.)

Although F. R. Leavis would become, with I. A. Richards and the American New Critics (Allan Tate, Robert Penn Warren, Cleanth Brooks, John Crowe Ransom, and William Empson), the scorn of post-1960s/1970s literary theory, *Scrutiny* was a project that sought to advance the rigor with how English literature was studied. Leavis subjected all he read, including Marxist literary criticism, to careful critique. A studious man, he read expansively, and he and Queenie not only kept *Scrutiny* an ongoing intellectual concern but also made it into a lodestar for interwar literary thinking. Leavis had, as we know from Ian MacKillop's brilliant 1995 biography of him, *F. R. Leavis: A Life in Criticism*, a voracious, assiduous, and studious mind.

What is more, even though Leavis may have lost the battle for the canon of literature (written in English), he won, hands down, the aesthetic one. Leavis is reputed to have been something of a dandy, a man renowned for his Romantic sensibility, always attired in fancy shirts, all ruffles, flamboyant collars, and cuffs. Lord Byron would have been envious.

"English" at Livingstone meant, as has been said, the canon. And what a remarkable and thorough initiation and immersion into the world of letters it was. Leavis or Brooks would have approved of it, and a figure such as C.L.R. James, educated in early twentieth-century Port of Spain, Trinidad, would certainly have nodded in recognition. The literary texts we studied would have been very familiar and welcome to James, who would have encountered a similar grounding in the canon in the classrooms of the prestigious Queens Royal College (QRC—where James would also teach, albeit briefly).

Morgan MacArthur (now Dr. Morgan Merrington), of Yorkshire origins, came to Livingstone via what was then Rhodesia after having secured a degree in English at UCT.

The canon and everything that turned on the literary were her mé-
tier, and then some. I learned the canon, joyously, in standards 8 and 9,
when Mrs. MacArthur introduced us to Shakespeare, Milton, the Romantics, the metaphysical poets (what a moment that was), the Victorian
Gerard Manley Hopkins ("The Windhover," truly an exercise in etymo-
logical minimalism), the modernists T. S. Eliot, Virginia Woolf, and so
on. To encounter the canon as a disenfranchised subject is, as Derrida
recounts of his education as a schoolboy in Algeria, to fall in love:

> I was confronting the truth of my geography lessons. But let that
> be. I shall content myself with a few allusions to literature. It is the
> first thing that I received from French education in Algeria, the
> only thing, in any event, that I enjoyed receiving. The discovery
> of French literature, the access to this so unique mode of writing
> that is called "French-literature" was the experience of a world
> without any tangible continuity with the one in which we lived,
> with almost nothing in common with our natural or social land-
> scapes.[2]

Above all, it was the discontinuity with apartheid lived reality that
inclined me so forcefully in the direction of the literary canon, a canon
that we knew as "English literature," our equivalent of Derrida's "French
literature." The truth of our geography lessons was, of course, apartheid,
a truth that Byron and Keats, or Napoleon, Otto von Bismarck and Ca-
millo Cavour in our history class, ruptured. Our "natural or social land-
scapes" differed greatly from those of George Eliot's *Middlemarch*; our
flora was distinct from Wordsworth's, our landscape bore little resemblance to the Mississippi of Mark Twain's *Huckleberry Finn*, although we
were a priori attuned to the racial elements of the relationship between
the runaway white boy Huck and the fugitive slave Jim. (We particularly
took note of how the young white boy holds the fate of the adult black
man in his hands. As much as Jim is worldly-wise and Huck is dependent
on his know-how, to a much greater extent is Jim at Huck's mercy. A single
word from Huck could literally be the end of Jim. Similarly, in apartheid
South Africa, the young white boy or girl had standing in the society;

the disenfranchised adult did not. The disenfranchised adult was compelled, by force of apartheid custom, always tinged with the threat of the law, to address the white child with an appropriate appellation: "Master," or in Afrikaans, "Klein Baas"—"Little Boss.") We could not help but be aware of the discordance, our "experience of a world without any tangible continuity," between the physical campus that was Livingstone and the European modernity that was the subject of our instruction.

But warm to the discovery of the literary canon I did, especially because literature opened worlds removed from ours, worlds that were unknown but not unknowable. Unlike the technical aspects of grammar that formed the core of our standard 6 syllabus, the hermeneutics of literature—"close analysis"—allowed the imagination to expand and freed the mind from the "truth of my geography lessons." What prepared us eminently for English classes with Mrs. MacArthur—Macky, out of earshot—is that we came to them after having been put through our paces by a teacher with whom we are already familiar, Peter Fiske, as fine an exponent of analyzing a poem as I have ever met.

Morgan MacArthur's taste in music, it seems to me, runs more in the direction of classical—Schubert, maybe, or Beethoven. Mozart might be too impetuous for her, too much given to excess and grandiosity. Regardless, Mrs. MacArthur did not possess the kind of cultural capital that generally appeals to adolescents bumbling about, stumbling this way and that, all the while trying to find their way in the world.

However, she is *that* English teacher, the one who used Gerald Durrell (*My Family and Other Animals* was the novel prescribed for our standard 8 reading; it gave us a glimpse of the madness of the itinerant English bourgeoisie in Corfu) and Wordsworth to expand our world well beyond the confines of 100 Lansdowne Road, the limits of the Cape Peninsula, and the borders of the Republic of South Africa. Mrs. MacArthur seemed to do this at every turn, whether she was teaching grammar or literature, opening the world through her keen sense of how to make the literary do other work.

She invited us, sometimes more subtly than others, to be done with the world of apartheid. She cajoled us to leave, if only temporarily, the land of apartheid, through whatever literary means we could, using as our means of exit whatever text there was to hand. More than that, she nudged us to take our first tentative steps beyond those texts prescribed by the CAD syllabus. She encouraged us to read, as did Mr. Fiske, authors near and far.

Among my fellow students was an early J. M. Coetzee devotee who thrilled to the release of *The Life and Times of Michael K*. This was 1977, and international honors for a South African author such as Coetzee were among the furthest things from anybody's mind at Livingstone. Coetzee would win a Nobel for literature in 2003. Appropriately, that fellow student went on to graduate from UCT, the same institution where Coetzee spent the vast majority of his teaching career, and become a high school English teacher. Coetzee long ago retired from UCT and now makes his home in Adelaide, Australia, a perfect city for cycling, his great passion. Formally or informally, Mrs. MacArthur secured the time for us to talk about these literary adventures. She licensed us to indulge our cultural pursuits and encouraged us to think against the strictures—literary, geopolitical—that the apartheid government was determined to impose.

We read *Romeo and Juliet* with her one year (standard 8), *Hamlet* and *Julius Caesar* the next. *Hamlet* remains my favorite piece of literature. When my son, Ezra, entered middle school in Ithaca, New York, he was assigned the play. While studying *Hamlet*, Ezra read Shakespeare's finest work twice a week with his tutor. Both Ezra and his tutor declared the language dated and pronounced the diction arcane, even though Ezra judged *ducats* to be the most apt term for money and mourns its untimely demise. Ezra and his tutor find Elizabethan English all rather inscrutable. I correct them, assuming the pose of mock despair. What know my American son and his American tutor of things so fine as Shakespeare? "Alas."

Charles Mills, the London-born Jamaican philosopher and author of the famed critique of liberalism as foundationally racist, *The Racial Contract*, passed away in September 2021. In his *New York Times* obituary,[3] Mills is shown to have favored J. R. Tolkien as a child. He read Tolkien, he impishly admitted, rather than Frantz Fanon, a much-venerated figure among black and anticolonial critics of all stripes.

Mills's affection for Tolkien put me in mind of Wordsworth's sonnet, "The World Is Too Much with Us." The core difficulty of Wordsworth's sonnet—humanity's alienation from Nature—lies in the second half:

> For this, for everything, we are out of tune;
> It moves us not.—Great God! I'd rather
> be
> A Pagan suckled in a creed outworn;
> So might I, standing on this pleasant lea
> Have glimpses that would make me less forlorn[4]

The poem bespeaks a disillusionment with humanity's alienation from Nature, but it also gave voice to, I recognize now, the possibility of a remove from what is. Through Mrs. MacArthur's teaching, we were made, in the best possible sense, "out of tune" with the apartheid world. We were made disjunctive with our physical and geopolitical environs. Wordsworth's was a provocation to make out of the moment of being forlorn a dialectical rupture. It was an urging not to be less forlorn but rather to be more so—and to be more so in order that we could gain access to glimpses of the world, a world where apartheid's proscriptions did not obtain. In order to inhabit that world, however, we had to make of apartheid's circumscription a thing "outworn." It may be that with every excursus into the canon of English literature, we were, little by little, "wearing" away at the fabric of our racist world. In other moments, however, we chafed against those strictures. It may be that, like Wordsworth's Toussaint, we had already pledged ourselves to the indestructible truth of the future:

> There's not a breathing of the common
> wind
> That will forget thee; thou hast great
> allies;
> Thy friends are exultations, agonies,
> And love, and man's unconquerable mind.[5]

Wordsworth's "To Toussaint L'Ouverture" did not make it onto the CAD syllabus. However, I later found the poem—or maybe it found me, and then not even directly. "To Toussaint L'Ouverture" presented itself to me as I worked my way through C.L.R. James's *The Black Jacobins*. Odd as it may at first seem, it may be that it is in Wordsworth that R. O. and Macky converged. It is more likely appropriate that my Livingstone teachers would converge here because what were William Blake and Wordsworth—together with Keats, the leading Romantic poets—if not lyricists of revolution? We are free to assert this, because we are familiar with Blake's recounting of "blood on palace walls"[6] and Wordsworth's trusting the truth of black history to the future, leaving it meanwhile in the capable hands of the "breathing of the common wind," "exultations," "agonies," and "love."

CAD's English syllabus was canonical, but always dialectically so. Alienation from Nature bears directly upon black revolution. Nevertheless, happening upon "To Toussaint L'Ouverture" was not part of the normal literary trajectory. The canon was, rather, full of Wordsworth's "daffodils," Robert Burns's "roses," Eliot's "smell of steak in passageways," and, of course, Shakespeare's meditations on love, especially in those sonnets.

After graduating from Livingstone, I would, as an English student at the then segregated UWC, add depth, Old English ("The Wanderer" and "The Seafarer"), medieval literature (*Sir Gawain and the Green Knight*; Chaucer's *Canterbury Tales*), and breadth (Milton's marvelously diabolical rendering of Lucifer; American literature, Emerson, Thoreau, Walt Whitman, Henry James) to my canonical store. At UWC, I would also study, for the first time in a formal setting, South African literature (Alan Paton, Athol Fugard, Guy Butler, Arthur Nortje, Nadine Gordimer; I would later supplement these with Jennifer Davids, Alex la Guma, Don Mattera, James Matthews) as well as African literature (Chinua Achebe, Wole Soyinka, Ngugi wa' Thiongo). As I was coming to the end of my UWC career, I would befriend Richard Rive, the subject of the final chapter, and it is Richard who would bridge these worlds, apartheid South Africa and newly sovereign black Africa, for me. A fiction writer, Rive, who belonged to the same generation of coloured authors as la Guma and Matthews, was deeply invested in opposing apartheid. In the

1950s and '60s, Rive traveled through Africa—as he would later travel to Europe, Asia, and North America—where he would become acquainted with writers such as Ngugi, Achebe, Soyinka, and Amos Tutuola, among other literary figures.

The effect of the works I read at UWC, most of which were new to me, was to make something of a fledgling postcolonial scholar of me. I was smitten with Ngugi's fiction (*A Grain of Wheat*, *Petals of Blood*, *Matigari*) but more so with his collection of essays, *Decolonizing the Mind*. I was entirely taken with Soyinka's drama (*Death and The King's Horseman*) and prose (*The Interpreters*); they promised entry to unknown horizons.

The notice board of UWC's English Department proudly displayed newspaper clippings about Soyinka's 1986 Nobel Prize. Everyone there took pride in Soyinka's triumph.

I was then, and remain so now, grateful to the canon that formed the basis of CAD instruction. I was indebted to it, really, if by indebted we understand there to be—and not in a pecuniary sense—a commitment or obligation to. The notion of debt, then, is integral to, constitutive of, and adds complexity to how gratitude is deployed in this writing. If "gratitude" bespeaks a feeling of being thankful for, then what "indebted" intensifies is the imperative, the obligation, to write the perverse truth of a BAD or CAD education, no matter that it was hardly experienced as such. The perversity, then, of acknowledging a debt, or indebtedness, is owed to that which intended to do violence to the disenfranchised. The intention—we might even designate it apartheid's commitment— to commit violence against disenfranchised minds remains in the spirit of the world that Wordsworth's "Toussaint" opened up. To owe is to make an accounting, no matter how perverse, unpleasant, and, indeed, heretical it might seem.

However, articulating such an obligation and owning up to so perverse a debt (that is, a debt that should not, under any circumstances, be named "debt") bring into public view a crucial recognition—at least potentially so. And the recognition is this: In the main, as Livingstone students, we are indebted to our teachers. We are obligated to them. It is their commitment to us, to invert the attribution, that has created in us a debt that is beyond recompense. (In any case, recompense to whom?) That is, it is precisely because this very notion of indebtedness played no role in their pedagogical calculations (an unfortunate turn of phrase, I readily admit). Their pedagogical commitment did nothing so much as disrupt any possibility of an economic calculus.

To render the matter poetically, their pedagogical commitment to us was born of their determination to make of their teaching a gift to us. That gift, I hasten to add, keeps on giving. The difficulties they posed, the unanswerable questions they proffered, the provocations they presented and then left dangling like bait are only the first delineation and acknowledgment of their bequest to us. Here, we see difficulty as the task that demanded attention above all else, the unanswerable question as the only question worth pondering, the provocation as the very seed of discomfiture. This gift is beyond calculation. It is the gift that compels itself into writing.

Because our teachers made of our minds an invaluable commodity (once more I fall prey to the language of economism), they were investing their various epistemologies and specializations (physics, history, English) in us without any expectation. They did not so much as ask for acknowledgment. They gave us, as far as they could, the world, or at least an opening onto the world.

Unbeknownst to her, Mrs. MacArthur used the canon to subversive and liberatory ends. It was a good thing, then, that the "world was so much with us; late and soon."[7] The world, she insisted by conscripting Wordsworth into revolution, was ours to be gained. It is appropriate to feel both thanks for and indebted to that gift.

It is no wonder, then, that I apprehend the canon as something other than oppressive. Though it was undoubtedly exclusionary, it did not oppress me—au contraire. And so I, disenfranchised though I was as I first encountered it, remain in its debt, regardless of all the furor that the canon wars provoked in the late 1980s and much of the 1990s, just as I was entering the U.S. academy as a graduate student. This was the moment of the "Killer Bs" in full attack mode. Allan Bloom (*The Closing of the American Mind*), Harold Bloom, and the openly racist Saul Bellow ("Show me the Zulu Tolstoy")[8] launched the opening salvoes in their attack on "political correctness," laying some of the groundwork for the critique of contemporary identity politics. (Constituted out of the afore-mentioned Blooms and Bellow, the Killer Bs were a group of conservative literary critics committed to the Western canon in its most exclusionary form. In the language of the day, the Killer Bs were viewed as gatekeepers of the canon as the singular preserve of Great White Men.)[9] The canon, however, I could not—and will never be able to—condemn to the dustbin of history because I am, and not only dialectically, in its debt and most likely always will be.

My indebtedness is such that it allows me to supersede whatever re-actionary (and exclusionary) tendencies the Killer Bs were espousing in defense of the canon. Bloom's attacks, wrongheaded as they were, had little to do with the effects reading Shakespeare, Keats, and Woolf had on disenfranchised students in apartheid South Africa.

To repeat, the logic of apartheid was circumscription. It involved making the world as small as possible for the disenfranchised and cutting them off from the rest of the world. The world stops, as it were, on the borders where South Africa met Mozambique, Botswana, and Zimbabwe. (Namibia was still effectively a colony known as South-West Africa.) In the constrictive and repressive logic of apartheid, the disenfranchised imaginary was a dangerous weapon. In the imaginary, no borders could be enforced. The mind was free to roam and was liberated to construct worlds it did not—was not supposed to—know. The imaginary was where apartheid met its limit. (What kind of imaginary urged Mills toward Tolkien? Surely no one expected the bookish Jamaican boy to acquaint himself with Fanon, certainly not in his teenage years. In declaring himself for Tolkien, was Mills mocking not only himself but also poking fun at the notion of what the intellectual archive of a postcolonial philosopher should be? Was he doing this from his earliest days—from his first encounter with the printed word or his first immersion in it?)

A few hours north of Cape Town, with its Mediterranean climate, lay a harsh landscape. The terrain was more befitting, some would suggest, the African hinterland. A dry, hard red soil, scarce vegetation, home to places such as Worcester and De Aar: That was the Karoo. That landscape and its vegetation I knew. I did not know daffodils until read I

Wordsworth. I had seen pictures of historic Athens but knew nothing about the splendor of Corfu until my classmates and I were led on a madcap journey through the Greek isles by Gerald Durrell's bohemian family. The grass, "Growing among black folks as among white"[10]—this was democracy, Walt Whitman–style. The powerful and hardly scrupulous Medicis, Michelangelo, and Leonardo da Vinci traversed history and English literature. Literature, more than any other subject except for history, opened up worlds for me that would otherwise have remained far beyond my ken. I admired the Kenyan-born writer Ngugi wa'Thiongo, but I am dialectical in relation to the canon rather than categorical, as in that moment when Karega, one of the four main protagonists in *Petals of Blood*, recounts the politics of the student strike at his high school, Siriana. Karega and his fellow students "wanted to be taught African literature, African history, for we wanted to know ourselves better. Why should we be reflected in in white snows, spring flowers fluttering by an icy lake?"[11] African literature and history should indeed have been a staple of a disenfranchised African child's education in apartheid South Africa. I, however, found in "white snows" and "spring flowers fluttering by an icy lake" an invitation to the disenfranchised South African mind to extend itself, to be, in a literary sense, outside itself. Everything else seems, under the conditions of a disenfranchised apartheid education, nothing more than a didactic fit of pique.

Taught in the way that Mrs. MacArthur did, the canon was nothing, in relation to the restrictions apartheid sought to impose, if not a vehicle for transgression. Such are the Augustinian workings of perversity. The world that seeks to deny provides the conditions that allow the subjugated to escape, to imagine their way out. An apartheid education was an object lesson in how to live—simultaneously and always dialectically—in more than one world. As I have written elsewhere, I left apartheid South Africa behind long before I boarded my first flight in August 1989. Bound for graduate school in the Unites States, I was already a world traveler courtesy of my CAD education, indefatigably still a neophyte in the business of crossing oceans, negotiating strange and strangely familiar lands.

What a good thing it is that the "world is too much with us."

What a world there was to gain, all because of an apartheid education. How perverse the effects of the education apartheid imposed upon the disenfranchised were.

Repetition

CAD education was premised on rote learning—multiplication tables, poems to be recited as part of the examination, important dates in history, how to conjugate German verbs (*Konjugieren das verb*: "*Ich bin, Du bist . . .*"). I can still, from memory, quote much of Hamlet's soliloquy in act 3 (is "To be or not to be"[12] not the very literary ground of Heidegger's *Sein und Zeit*?), I continue to hold up Marc Antony's oration as the greatest political speech in history (how anarchically Marc Antony turns Caesar's "grievous" ambition into an indictment of the "noble Brutus"),[13] and I can recite most if not all of Rudyard Kipling's "If—" under pain of death ("If you can keep your head about you . . .").[14]

If a CAD pupil was going to lose his head anywhere in the morass and mediocrity that apartheid education was intent on creating, then Morgan MacArthur's English class was by far the best place to do so.

Out of Morgan MacArthur's class there would emerge, in short order, medical professionals (a doctor currently practicing in Canada; a radiologist in Australia), an attorney ("advocate," in South African parlance), and several teachers—preeminently English teachers, as one would expect (the Coetzee devotee among them, of course).

The way in which Morgan MacArthur presented the literary to our English class brings to mind Deleuze and Guattari's phrase "lines of flight," a proposition that offers a philosophical mode through which we might map a different world. In the late 1970s, CAD pupils at institutions such as Livingstone and in classes such as those taught by Peter Fiske, Morgan MacArthur, and R. O. Dudley were invited to follow those lines of flight, no matter how fanciful an undertaking it might have seemed.

It was little wonder, then, that Mrs. MacArthur is undoubtedly the teacher who, together with Richard Owen Dudley, had the greatest intellectual impact on me at Livingstone.

Mr. Dudley has gone now. I still occasionally talk with Dr. Merrington.

I always address her, however, as "Mrs. MacArthur."

Somewhere in my thinking, it is still 1979. And if it is 1979, then I am disenfranchised. If it is 1979, then I am delighting, as I have ever since, in *Hamlet*. That is why my address to my English teacher is, as it always will be, anachronistic.

What my anachronism allows is for me take a perverse pleasure in the realization that the time—Hamlet's and mine—is out of joint. What a thing it is to be, contrary to Wordsworth's lament, out of tune. What a thing it is that the world of Livingstone is still, at least here, in this account, with us. This world has been rendered as faithfully as possible, which is to say that it hews to a truth—to the truth that the English teacher, a daughter of Yorkshire and a purveyor of the canon, presented to her charges. This world is one in which at least one of her students, although there are surely many more, remains gratefully saturated.

Without that world Livingstone, no other worlds would be imaginable.

How could there have been, given this outcome, no debt incurred? Through indebtedness comes intellectual liberation. What is it that was incubated in such a glorious indebtedness? Thinking. This type of thinking, patinaed with the same impishness as Charles Mills's mischievous affection for Tolkien, is a perversity.

In all this, Mills and I find ourselves not in the least unique. Our perversity, such as it is, if it can indeed be named perversity, is simply the latest iteration of a dialectical gratitude that stretches all the way to that old QRC boy. We remember that "Thackeray, not Marx," as James notes in *Beyond a Boundary*, "bears the heaviest responsibility for me."

And so a politically confounding lineage, as ideologically dubious as it is alluring and as conducive to producing a searing internal conflict as it is to giving the reader pleasure (Thackeray, not Marx; Tolkien, not Fanon; Shakespeare, not Trotsky), manifests itself. It is, however, by no means an exclusionary lineage. It is, to the very last, dialectical.

It is never, you see, Thackeray or Marx, Tolkien or Fanon.

It is—always—*and*, out of which an entirely new urgent and thought-provoking dialectic presents itself.

"Worlds are too much with us."[15]

The difficult and engaging tensions inherent to the conjunction of worlds may, when all is said and done, be the most fecund breeding grounds for thinking.

Once more, we recall Heidegger: *"Denke est Danke."*

Thinking is thanking. We return later to the unbreakable bond between thinking and thanking that Heidegger forged for us.

For now, however, it behooves us only to keep Heidegger's conjoining in mind.

Alles gut.[16]

Interlude II

Postapartheid Education, Unconcealed

With the institution of the universal franchise in 1994, education would no longer be segregated, although South African education steadfastly remains a vastly unequal enterprise. The difference is, as is common of the postcolonial (or postapartheid), the children of the formerly colonized or oppressed now have access to the same educational institutions—and their concomitant privileges—as the historical white ruling class.

In truth, the story of postapartheid education is a depressing one in no small measure because it is so predictable and, as such, eminently avoidable. "Alas, poor Yorick,"[1] Mrs. MacArthur might have been moved to ruefully remark. It is akin to the failed promise that leaves Karega, in the wake of his expulsion from Siriana, somewhere "between despair and dumb comprehension."[2]

In August 2018, at the end of a visit to Cape Town, I walked by Livingstone and decided to enter the school grounds. I know not what I intended to do there; perhaps I was looking for the ghosts of my younger self, nostalgic for a time gone by. Alas, I found only sad specters. I suppose I can say that as I wandered through Livingstone's passageways and my old classrooms, I would have been grateful for an attack of anamnesis. Denied anamnesis, I would happily have settled for at least a healthy dose of "obliterine" and "amnesol," ironically—but not so ironically that the inference and humor might be missed—named drugs that Stanislaw Lem prescribes for doing away with memory in his novel *The Futurological Congress*. The intellectual intensity that marked my everyday life there was patently, tragically absent. Pathos prevailed.

In 2018, Livingstone was not (yet) slovenly or unkempt, but there was a sloppiness about the place. During my walkabout, I noticed that what Livingstone lacked was the kind of attention to housekeeping detail to which I had been accustomed in my tenure there. The hallways, the quad, and the garden had been kept in good order, if not immaculate. There had been no candy or gum wrappers littering the entryway, no papers fluttering across the quad. A clean, well-kept campus had been the rule when I was there.

Founded in 1926, Livingstone is an old institution. The physical plant has expanded in the intervening decades. Now the school even has its own auditorium, a facility not even dreamt of when I was there. But in 2018, Livingstone felt old, or, more accurately, older. My disappointment, if that is the correct term, might of course be nothing other than the nostalgia of an old boy returning to find his adolescent haunts much altered.

However, I realized that my out-of-placeness in relation to the current instantiation of the institution had nothing to do with either my wistfulness or simple chronology—the inevitable passing of the years. I would rather not enter Livingstone High School again, especially now, as it nears its centenary. I would rather my teachers, Richard Owen Dudley above all, because he is without a doubt the greatest teacher to ever grace those halls, be spared such a fate too. I could not bear to see Livingstone submit to a creeping decrepitude. The spirit of the school now weaker than the body.

Autoimmunity

After all, it was at Livingstone that we were educated into autoimmunity even as rote learning, through endless repetition, predominated under apartheid's CAD. Perhaps it is because of all that repetition that we were instructed into autoimmunity. This is appropriate, one might say, because autoimmunity reminds us that the very thing that protects us will, at some point or other, reveal itself as the cause of our destruction.

Apartheid—that system that so unapologetically sought to under- or miseducate the disenfranchised, the system designed to abjure, renounce, repudiate, render thinking impossible—made nothing so obvious or important as the absolute need for thinking. This need was grounded not only, as it should have been, in history, but in a soil more profound, fecund and, indeed, Socratic. Livingstone trained its students to think in order to know how to live—to know how to live under the strictures of apartheid and to think about how to *Be* under apartheid.

In this regard, there is something about Plato's *Phaedrus* that haunts. That is because in this dialogue, Plato recounts the clarity of Socrates's thinking, a thinking made all the more powerful and poignant because it is a dialogue that takes place as Socrates is about to be put to death by the hemlock contained in the poisoned chalice. In order to know how to die, Socrates says, we must have known how to live so that we could prepare ourselves for death. We are learning to live in order to know how to die.[3] Livingstone taught generations of students a rather distinct Socratic lesson: To learn how to live in order to think a life freed of the institutional strictures, existential threats, and deep antipathy to—fear of?—thinking that was disenfranchised apartheid education.

To live inclined toward Being, such an inclining could only begin, Livingstone teachers intuited (even if they did not explicitly, and certainly not articulately, state as much) by thinking (simultaneously from within and against) a pedagogical bureaucracy structured to impede thinking at every turn. Under these dialectical conditions, there was nothing for Livingstone faculty and students to do but struggle with themselves pedagogically, politically. Livingstone was an institution at once opposed to and constrained by apartheid; simultaneously subject to CAD strictures and chafing against it; at once dependent on CAD resources and bitterly opposed to the restrictions apartheid law imposed on it through its CAD directives and the CAD surrogates—regional inspectors, departmental officials, and so on—who were free to impose their authority on the institution.

Locked, then, into ceaseless contestation between resistance (a sub-version-through-pedagogy) and compliance (a pedagogy-in-conformity), between adhering to the CAD syllabus and undermining it, Livingstone instantiates, in the terms of that peculiarly Sartrean dialectics, "negative thought."

Repetition

A great deal of the CAD syllabus turned on rote learning. Most subjects—mathematics ($7 \times 7 = 49$), declension, parts of speech, geography (Mount Kilimanjaro is the highest mountain in Africa), and history (South Africa was "discovered" in 1652)—involved the memorization of facts.

It is a strange irony that the last four digits of my telephone number are 1652.

Today, I am still able to recall these facts, although by tenth grade, mathematics and I had gone our separate ways. It was a mutually beneficial divorce; mathematics, no doubt, was relieved to be rid of me, and I of it.

Many of the expensively educated American and international students I have taught over the past three decades have only the scantest command of world geography and know only the barest history; much of what they do know is, at best, provincial. The world, and how it came to be constituted as it is, appears to be of little interest to them. Their world, for all its tech-savviness, appears to be at once unreflectively global and embarrassingly local.

I sometimes gently mock my students today by calling them the "global elite."

I am grateful to my apartheid education.

At Livingstone, we chafed at rote learning, but we mastered our multiplication and division tables, we made our acquaintance with far-off lands (thereby expanding our geopolitical horizons, making the world a place we desired to know more keenly), and we became intimately familiar with major historical figures—imperious Napoleon; cagey, pragmatic Bismarck; brave, determined Garibaldi; the hapless but brutal Czar Nicholas II.

We developed a strong antipathy toward the Dutch East India Company's Jan van Riebeeck, who "founded" a colony at the Cape of Good Hope, and Simon van der Stel, the second governor of the colony and the architect of the castle that still stands at the southwestern edge of downtown Cape Town. A sense of biliousness marked our every encounter with the antidemocratic, blatantly racist Voortrekkers, who abandoned the Cape Colony and ventured north after the British government abolished slavery.

I simplify the conditions that produced the Great Trek, but I do know that we correctly identified in those white colonists the antecedents of the apartheid regime that took power a century later, in 1948. We could date the first iterations of the ideology that would become apartheid. History, as Marx so famously intoned in the "Eighteenth Brumaire of Louis Bonaparte," repeats itself, first as tragedy, then as farce. We found ourselves caught in Marx's first cycle—tragedy—living the repetition of that nineteenth-century ideology as high school students more than a hundred years later. To my mind, the "Eighteenth Brumaire" is Marx's funniest, most astringent piece of writing. One almost winces, so sharply does Marx lampoon Napoleon's grubby, clueless nephew. I hoped that we would never have to live history as farce. Contemporary postapartheid South Africa has proved tragic enough for the nation's recently enfranchised blacks; the adage *the more things change, the more they stay the same* in large measure reflects the fate of historically disenfranchised South Africans.

We learned through repetition and after having been incessantly made to memorize, never to forget.

We were never to forget that which was so forcefully imposed upon us as "history." We became critics, occasionally even articulate ones, of what CAD education sought to pass off as scientific truth. We knew this to be a "truth" lacking all veracity. The truth of our present reminded us of this falsehood, often on a daily basis. We would not be held prisoner by apartheid's regime of veridiction.

We learned through repetition. Somewhere Hegel says that we learn only through rote, *auswendig*, and Paul de Mann has real regard for memorization, *Gedächtnis*. I find myself in happy and grateful agreement.

CAD education is "negative" in the sense that the operative conditions are, at once and by turns, proscriptive and generative. The dialectic that emerged out of this anti-apartheid apartheid education did not produce, as might be expected, "an unhappy consciousness" (Hegel's term). What it did instead was reveal an intellectual fecundity that was always in struggle, even sometimes with itself, as it sought to determine what was pedagogically (and politically) permissible and worried about when to be strident in its opposition, when to interrogate in a lower register, and, most difficult, when to comply with the regime's dictates. A demanding business, this is, the work of decision. The intellectual fecundity turned—for the anti-apartheid self—turbulent when teachers, students, and the community took up the work of resisting apartheid from within the educational apparatus. There were boycotts, strikes, and marches, as well as a recognition that passing examinations and achieving accreditation from within and through the CAD were modes of struggle that were umbilically connected. Living in these conditions reminds one of W.E.B. Du Bois's description of a Negro's "two-ness . . . two souls, two thoughts, two unreconciled strivings; two warring ideals in one dark body, whose dogged strength alone keeps it from being torn asunder."[4] Two warring souls are compelled into a conflict, and it is only through enduring—a term that only begins to describe the contention that is the work of surviving a conflict to which the self commits itself—the conflict that another mode of life can be made possible. Under this new life, pedagogy is not the everyday site of struggle and certainly not an ongoing source of conflict that requires such an inordinate amount of "strength" to keep the self from being "torn asunder."

However, no matter the difficulty of trying to be while facing the prospect of being torn asunder, that struggle within and against contained within the condition that was BAD, CAD, and IAD education was an autoimmune kernel that blended anamnesis with an incipient perversity of gratitude—an autoimmune kernel in which anamnesis and the perversity of gratitude came, as they should have, into unflinching conflict.

Autoimmunity, then, as the catalyst for an impropriety that insists, without hesitation, upon the sovereignty of its name. So conceived, *The Perversity of Gratitude* constitutes a history of anti-apartheid pedagogy in which everything—every thinking of apartheid and its educational apparatus (and all that maintained it)—derives from a concept, the perversity of gratitude, that is contrary to all political expectation. This is less a Gramscian history from below and more a history of the philosophically obvious, an obviousness that owes everything to a palimpsestic dialectic, if such an unwieldy analogy might be permitted.

As we know, Livingstone's Latin motto is *Nulla vestige retrosum*—"No footsteps backward." In this declarative, there is the refusal to retreat in the face of apartheid and anti-apartheid commonsense, which holds that the apartheid-era education offered the disenfranchised a substandard education (which in so many respects it did, often with a bureaucratic and repressive edge that can only be described as sadistic). *The Perversity of Gratitude* stands against such commonsense—unflinchingly, without apology. The terms upon which *The Perversity of Gratitude* stands are unambiguous: Disenfranchised apartheid education constituted fertile ground for thinking. As such, the perversity of gratitude writes anti-apartheid pedagogy as, in Benedetto Croce's sense ("all history is contemporary history"),[5] the history of the present. It is the history of how thinking was autoimmunely lodged at the core of disenfranchised education. This is a history that could only be written in and out of a present—following and reinforcing Croce's dictum—that lays determined claim to a thinking that emerged then, without acknowledgment, in disenfranchised schools.

That CAD or BAD schools were a hotbed of thinking was in no way recognized by the ruling NP. At best, the apartheid regime denounced any opposition, school boycott, student protest, or pedagogical defiance as, among other things, communist agitation—the work, surely, of teachers who were clearly Marxist provocateurs. In fairness, it is not so much that the NP government was wrong on this score. There was certainly agitation enough, in one guise or another, at BAD, CAD, and IAD schools. It is, rather, that the apartheid regime was insufficiently Heideggerian. Thinking, as so carefully attended to by Heidegger, was an undertaking beyond the regime's (philosophical) ken.

In recognition of that, what could be more appropriate—proper, *propre*, *echt*, *behoorlike*—than to grant favor to the education apartheid imposed upon the disenfranchised. Once more, we return to the Heideggerian injunction *"Denken est Danke"*—"thinking is thanking." (In Afrikaans, Heidegger's German rendering echoes resonantly, even if the translation is slightly more wordy, imbuing the Afrikaans language with a new poetry: *"Om te dink is te dank."* However, I can say with certainty that no such phrase, to say nothing of the concept, has ever graced the Afrikaans language.) Understood in Heidegger's terms, we find ourselves confronted—or is that hoisted by our own petard?—by a new and resonant autoimmunity. The essential argument that presents itself to us, as this work seeks to make clear, is that it is proper rather than perverse to express gratitude for those historical forces that incline us toward thinking. Were we to extend our argument to its outermost limits, we could say that it is only through an engagement with that which is presumed perverse that we happen upon a discomfiting truth. Thinking is as likely to emerge out of conditions that appear historically most unsuited for and resistant to it. Indeed, to risk ourselves even more, we can say that there is a perverse correlation between abjuration and thinking—in short, a dialectic. The more abjure the conditions, the more the conditions lend themselves to thinking. The need for thinking is never so acute as when the conditions under which it must manifest itself abjure thinking. And if philosophy is for Heidegger nothing other than the work of thinking, then to think under apartheid was "to have sight for what is essential."[6]

While the conditions for thinking are hardly ever optimal, the need to think can thrive where least expected. To think under these conditions is to reach for or retrieve that which is "essential." To possess such "sight" is to turn the self in the direction of thinking. That such a coming to life, such an inclining toward the essential, is even possible speaks not only to the resilience at the core of thinking but also to the perverse nature of thinking.

Having come to thinking along this perverse path, is it possible to suggest that generations of Livingstone students were more inclined to thinking than their contemporaries at well-resourced and superbly maintained (institutions that knew none of the material lack experienced at BAD, CAD, and IAD schools) white schools? While white institutions, with their vastly superior resources, could present their students with far greater access to knowledge (*savoir*), under no circumstances must we confuse such access as guaranteeing a more direct route to thinking, nor must knowledge—or even command of knowledge—be mistaken for thinking. (By itself, savoir is often the mark of what Sartre considers the "false intellectual." It is only by "situating" knowledges,[7] especially in relation to the working classes, Sartre insists, that the intellectual can arrive at her or his truth.) Our white contemporaries were epistemologically advantaged by apartheid, but their superior access to savoir set them on a "false path." They had far greater access to resources that allowed them to expand their systems of knowledge. (Sartre, before Foucault, is the thinker to directly link knowledge to power, if only in a negative sense, because for Sartre, bourgeois "technicians of knowledge" were regarded as inconsequential by those who wielded power. Under apartheid, however, we were no match for our white contemporaries in this regard. They would have direct access to power. They would, in fact, instantiate it. They would become captains of industry and political leaders, all walks of life from which we were systematically excluded. Under apartheid, in this sense, Department of Education knowledge was power. As disenfranchised students, what we clung to reveals nothing so much as the value we assigned our anti-apartheid apartheid education. It is no wonder that the phrase "They can take everything from you, except your education" obtained with such resoluteness—no matter that it was overwritten with precisely the fear that even education itself was no guarantee against the violence of apartheid—and stubborn hope in the ranks of the disenfranchised, serving as an obligation stubbornly passed from one CAD-educated generation to the next. However, this truth does nothing to reduce the vulnerability of our condition. As importantly, it speaks of the desperation of our situation as disenfranchised students—and disenfranchised subjects in general—who held fast to our education when we were stripped of all else.) However, while constitutive of thinking, epistemology does not itself rise to the level of thinking; epistemology by itself doth not thinking make.

On this distinction, Heidegger is at once declarative and nuanced. Knowledge can contribute to thinking, maybe even crucially so, and it could even lead to thinking, but it is not thinking itself. To know is not to think. Inversely, to know—intuit—that there is a great deal more to know (which is always the case) and that what there is to know is deliberately and unjustly being denied one might, as a constitutive lack, prove generative in relation to thinking. Is it possible that thinking what cannot, because of structural racism, be known might itself produce a greater aptitude for and openness to thinking? Out of epistemological lack comes thinking. Rendered formulaically, the more knowledge is withheld from the disenfranchised, the more inclined the *savoir*-deficient are to thinking?

A thought, a series of thoughts, or, more properly, a series of provocations surely bears scrutiny and must be made a subject for thinking precisely because it presents so perverse a proposition.

Such a proposition accords with what Louis Althusser presents, in his *Reading Marx*, as "causal" or "structural effectivity," which he traces to "'*Darstellung*,'" the key epistemological concept of the whole Marxist theory of value—the concept whose object is precisely to designate the mode of presence of the structure in its effects and therefore to designate structural causality itself.[8]

The entire structure of apartheid, including its laws, its Department of Education, and its ideology writ large, was "present" in each and every BAD and CAD school. Its "effects" manifested themselves everywhere (in the curriculum, in the principals it appointed, in the structural deficiency, in the very location of the school itself)—less, we might suggest, as a "mode of presence" than Benthamite ubiquity, in all its unsubtlety.

The effect of the whole of that apartheid state (and its manifold apparatuses) is best apprehended, then, in terms of how its effects could be detected in the various constituent parts that we know—in this case, as BAD, CAD, and IAD. This effect is made all the more revealing if we recognize that those constituent parts are not equal. BAD ≠ CAD ≠ IAD, and none of these are individually or collectively equal to the Department of Education. Sometimes what distinguishes one disenfranchised institution is not so much the quality of the teacher, the location of the school (under apartheid, not all institutions were "equal" in their physical site or location), or even the disenfranchised students' aptitude for learning; instead, it was what we might refer to as, in the terms advanced by Deleuze and Guattari, the intensity that saturates the institution. The greater the intensity, the greater the chance for thinking to become possible. All the while, of course, we must acknowledge how difficult it is to properly define *intensity*.[9] Though this rendering is incomplete, suffice it to say that *intensity* is that mode of apprehension formed out of a committed pedagogy, a student body trained to be highly receptive to learning what is put before them formally (the syllabus), to think intuitively in the direction of what might be, to take a critical institutional approach to epistemology (always tuned to the effect of material lack but never restrained or defeated by unequal access to resources), and, most importantly of all in this case, to be inclined toward thinking, which cannot be undertaken without intellectual focus, discipline, and a stringent openness of mind.

That is how, in my recollection, intensity made itself immanent at Livingstone.

In attending to "effects," we are able to, in the spirit of Deleuze and Guattari, leave aside what always seems to be the first question (as posed by hermeneutics, as if it were a question on the order of the exegetical)—"What does it mean?"—in order to take up the more urgent and generative line of inquiry: "How does it work?"[10]

Apartheid education for the disenfranchised "worked" to produce, as an unintended consequence (in some disenfranchised institutions of learning more obviously than others, never consistently, and always dialectically), thinking. Deleuze and Guattari's preferred question pertains to the "problem of peopling in the unconscious,"[11] but it functions, in this instance, as a double-edged sword, if we can make of the sword solely a Janus-faced interrogative. As such, the question is not only *How does apartheid education work?*; it is also *How is it the disenfranchised came to undertake the work of thinking?*

Concepts 3

Thinking a Debt

Thinking a debt in the aftermath of apartheid is, to follow Alain Badiou's evental logic of supplementarity,[1] to think in the moment that is not that which gave birth to this logic of perversity, this perverse gratitude.

To have lived under apartheid made thinking—thinking against apartheid, thinking for what might succeed it—an intellectual imperative. To live under apartheid was, on a daily basis, because of the potential humiliations that attended the most routine exercise (going to school, visiting a hospital, taking public transportation, and so on), to understand the imperative for thinking in order to stay alive in the world of apartheid. Again, the perversity announces itself, this time rendered as a maxim: Apartheid was made for thinking. Rendered temporally, apartheid is the time for thinking. To temporalize apartheid as thinking is to at once enact an intellectual appropriation (to claim apartheid for thinking, which is precisely what the white minority regime opposed through those institutions we know as acronyms—CAD, etc.) and insist that it is under the most dire historical circumstances (here Agamben's all-purpose notion of the "camp" is of notional use) that thinking is most impera-tive, that thinking is what is needed first, not last.[2]

Out of this perversity, we can posit, as a declarative, at least the following claim. The time of apartheid presented—to extend and, as such, test the limits of the metaphor of perversity—not only the necessary but the ideal conditions for thinking. The thinking that emerged under the conditions of apartheid could not have, reduc-tively phrased, been produced under any other conditions, and the very institutions that sought to make thinking secondary if not impos-sible were, contrary to the cynical intentions of the architects of apartheid education, nothing other than *ideal*—that word again, per-versely invoked—incubators for thinking. To borrow that famous title from James Agee and Walker Evans, perverted, of course: "Let us now praise the famous architects of apartheid education."[3] And how far from praise is thanks?

Think about the value of education, and not just in material terms—that is, through a critique of the vastly different and unequal sums spent on white, coloured, black, or Indian children, to use the terminology of the day. The very acronyms, perhaps only conceiv-able under the sign of apartheid, can be understood as a perverse gift because that which was denied and was made available un-equally in terms of the law served the dialectical purpose of both assailing the fact of gutter education (which would have begun, out of historical necessity, from the difference in currency disburse-ment—so many rands for whites, so many for Indians, and so on, in ever-decreasing amounts) and of imagining, positing, and arguing over what would constitute an education fit for a citizen rather than a racialized, racially oppressed being. If this was not "education for barbarism" (to revisit the words of Tabata), then what kind of educa-tion was it? What kind of education would meet the needs of the citizen? Specifically, what kind of education would meet the needs of the citizen who has not—who cannot, because history will not allow it—forgotten the experience of "inferior education," another moni-ker from a time gone by (but a moniker, I suspect, whose time has not passed within the postapartheid nation's borders or education system; the stratification continues, unabated, perhaps as class rather than race becomes the chief instrument of division)?

The Diaspora-in-Place

Because apartheid educated me, it produced yet one more unintended consequence. Because apartheid taught me to think, it provided me safe passage out of the country before I ever set foot outside of South Africa. CAD education included in its syllabi the geography of African countries, especially that of our southern African neighbors—Rhodesia (before it became Zimbabwe), Botswana, Angola, Mozambique, South-West Africa (before it became Namibia; at the time, it was still under South African rule). CAD education insisted that we know the history of the two World Wars. Our English classes introduced us to, as noted earlier, Shakespeare, Milton, Keats, the metaphysical poets, and Gerald Durrell's *My Family and Other Animals*; they familiarized us with the Romanticism of Wordsworth's "lonely clouds" and "daffodils" as well Blake's revolutionary urgings that could be detected in the soldiers "sigh/Runs in blood down palace walls,"[4] and as disenfranchised students, we were transported out of South Africa. Our CAD education gave us access to another world, a world beyond the racist strictures and systemic circumscriptions of apartheid.

Because of our CAD education, we were free to leave. We were free to leave Livingstone, our segregated neighborhoods on the Cape Flats, Cape Town, and South Africa itself. We were free to think ourselves in another world—a world free of apartheid. Our CAD education diasporized us. It threw us out into the world, if we follow Heidegger's notion of "thrownness"—the exposure of the self to the world, a casting of the self into the world that is always subject to randomness.

Today there are graduates of the class of 1980 all over the world. The vast majority of my classmates have remained in South Africa. However, I know that some of those I have kept track of have dispersed across the world. There are some in Australia and at least one in Canada. One spent some time in New Zealand before return-ing to a bucolic hamlet a few hours outside Cape Town. There at least two in Germany, one of whom moved there after teaching in the Emirates. There are most likely others living abroad. Of those I know who emigrated, most are medical professionals (as previously noted) and teachers.

As the Livingstone school song goes:

We may roam the wide world over
We may scale the highest peak
We may stake our claim to wealth or fame
Whatever end we seek
But we always will remember the school whose aim has been
"Nulla vestige retrosum"

And roam we have, the class of 1980.

But that is the story of migration—of physically leaving South Africa.

The diaspora-in-place is different. It is a deracination of the mind. It is the process by which a historical subject remains physi-cally in place but already lives, in terms of how they understand the world and what their frame of reference is, somewhere else.

The diaspora-in-place is having left a place before one physi-cally removes oneself from this place.

I left South Africa a long time before I boarded a plane, for the very first time, in August 1989. I was gone long before I left. Com-plications attend to living the diaspora-in-place. It is an odd admix-ture of ignorance and knowledge. When living somewhere other than where one physically resides, there is the sense—a life made and sus-tained in the mind—that one already knows another place before one has physically set foot there. One is then confronted with the vast ignorance that comes from living so "abstractly" in this place where one has never physically been. Nevertheless, to live the dias-pora-in-place is to throw oneself into a mode of being in the world that—no matter the difficulties of everyday physical reality in that place against which one chafes, which one resists—has the effect of presenting to the self a world more livable, a world more in tune with how one wants to be in the world. (Again, Heidegger, the randomness, chance and the unexpected are all constitutive of thrownness.)

This is how the knowledge accrued through a CAD education (about Europe, its wars, America, its wars, Africa, its agriculture) sustains the self in the face of apartheid and then prepares the self for the actual experience of physically inhabiting cities such as Canberra or New York. This is how German acquired in a CAD high school allows one to adjust to Berlin.

The diaspora-in-place, however, is not only to leave without having left. It is also the impossibility of leaving despite having left.

The CAD- or BAD-educated disenfranchised self will never be free of the place from which that self sought to extricate itself, from which it sought and found refuge elsewhere, only to find that there can be no severing of the psychological umbilical cord that binds the disenfranchised self to that place itself. The diaspora-in-place always returns, and most often in the least expected or desired moments, to remind the disenfranchised self that its physical relocation is no match for the ties that bind it so indissolubly to that very place it was so determined to leave—and to leave behind. The diaspora-in-place is (made) perverse because of that indestructible tie.

Having been able to live elsewhere without actually being elsewhere, I can say the reverse now turns out to be equally true. Having liberated itself physically, the disenfranchised self now finds that so much of itself remains *there* (apartheid South Africa). That *there* now shows itself to be even more resilient than the original diaspora-in-place—that *there* has now taken up permanent, unshakable residence in the disenfranchised's *here* (Canberra, Berlin, New York). It is as though the physically diasporized disenfranchised self finds itself the subject of a cruel Eagles joke. To live diasporized after having lived (escaped?) the condition of sustaining the self through life of the diaspora-in-place is to know the truth of the diaspora-in-place as rendered in "Hotel California": "You can check out, but you can never leave."[5] Unbeknownst to them, Don Henley and Glenn Frey (who wrote the lyrics)[6] always provide the soundtrack to the concept that is the diaspora-in-place: "And I was thinking to myself/'This could be Heaven or this could be Hell.'" Or, it could be both or neither; by turns, it could be one and then the other. But "checking out" of this condition is never possible.

In a perverse way, what the diaspora-in-place brings into thinking is that the historically disenfranchised subject owes its apartheid education an unintended debt. Being able to live the diaspora-in-place is due entirely to apartheid. Phrased cynically, the disenfranchised was able to leave apartheid South Africa free of charge—any fiscal charge, that is. The disenfranchised can never be properly compensated for the many other costs that attend to living the diaspora-in-place. Nevertheless, a debt has been created. The piper must be paid.

And the charge issued by thinking must always be addressed.

Only thinking can do the work of thinking.

Nur Denken kann die Arbeit des Denkens leisten: can achieve the work of thinking.

Nur Denken kann die Arbeit des Denkens tun: can do the work of thinking.

Nur Denken kann die Arbeit des Denkens vollziehen: can realize the work of thinking.

An injunction so uncompromising it demands several iterations.

The Unconscious of Gratitude

Gratitude, perversely construed, must have a critical function—that is, a dialectical function, one that is necessarily negative. It is only through the perversity of gratitude that it becomes possible, to borrow the terms Jameson offers in *The Political Unconscious*, to "restore to the surface of the text the repressed and buried reality of [its] fundamental history."[7] Rather than merely restore, the perversity of gratitude reinstates—and not only at the level of the surface—and excavates a fundamental aspect of anti-apartheid history. The perversity of gratitude brings to light—what Heidegger names the clearing—what we might, here again invoking Jameson, take as the grateful unconscious (or, no matter that it lacks Jameson's signature poetic touch, the unconscious of gratitude). Indeed, to not speak the unconscious of gratitude is to make of the disenfranchised's apartheid education—BAD, CAD, and IAD in their structural entirety—an impregnable behemoth. To not acknowledge the unconscious of gratitude is to make of a Livingstone student something akin to, at best, a *pensée sauvage*—a wild and undisciplined thinker. It would be better if we were understood as Sartrean "monsters," not in Sartre's Romanticized sense (as intellectuals who stand outside the entire apparatus of the state) but rather as the "monstrous products of a monstrous society," thinking beings compelled, by our "monstrous society" (the ongoing racism of the apartheid regime), to oppose it with a "monstrous" energy that derives out of the "true" intellectual's capacity to "disquiet" society.[8] Such a monster goes, as Shakespeare would have it, by the name of Caliban and is possessed of a Hegelian "unhappy consciousness." This monster is liberated into anticolonial consciousness by Prospero's occupation of his island. Caliban comes to know the bitterness of being entrapped in and by the colonizer's language. Caliban knows that perverse historical condition under which his "reason" came to be. Caliban knows how it is he came to possess the only language in which he can speak his dissent. Caliban's dependence on and immersion in the language of the colonizer is among the chief sources of his anger at his overlord Prospero: "You taught me language; and my profit on't / Is, I know how to curse; the red plague rid you, / For learning me your language."[9] Out of so variable and many-headed a "monstrosity" arises thinking. Out of this "paradox," as Du Bois names it, there emerges the "black *savant*."[10] The black being comes to think under all manner of conditions—Shakespearean drama, the Sartrean Gothic (which sets itself so determinedly against the lure of technicity that is bourgeois knowledge), the pathos that is Du Bois's double-consciousness. This is how a perverse gratitude is, as Caliban would insist, ever conscious of his subjugation, "learned." To live in language is, as such, to know the contradiction that brings Caliban into history. After Prospero is usurped by his brother, Antonio, from his rightful inheritance (to become Duke of Milan), his imperial misadventure spawns, across the centuries, a succession of Calibans. One after the other, they all draw from the same self-reflection-inducing well that is Caliban's "cursed language," all endeavoring, always unsuccessfully, to be rid of that which plagues them so relentlessly. All are intimately familiar with the "curse" of a perverse gratitude.

To refuse, then, the unconscious of gratitude is to reify the disenfranchised's apartheid education. It would, as such, be tantamount to a historical failure because it cannot recognize how the pedagogical work (and political instruction, let us be clear) of anti-apartheid teachers was instrumental in undoing apartheid education through dialectical legerdemain or how it was the pedagogical commitment of anti-apartheid teachers in a school such as Livingstone that enabled them to develop a "pedagogical mechanism" (dispositif pédagogique, a set of pedagogical devices) to both meet the structural requirements of the CAD syllabus and to supplement or undermine that same syllabus.[11] Sometimes both occurred, a consequence of using the same pedagogical device.

A history lesson that countered the official narrative of South Africa, a Wordsworth poem ("London," with its "blood down palace walls") transposed in time and place, an Afrikaans lesson that invoked banned authors (e.g., Breyten Breytenbach), all derived from the same pedagogical device, always a double-edged means of instruction. The genius of the dialectical resides not only in its ability to emerge in unexpected moments (thus making of itself an event); it resides equally in its ability to operate in confined spaces or to shape-shift so much so as to make itself unrecognizable as intellectual subversion because it hews, at least ostensibly, so closely to the official narrative. Dialectical legerdemain is the very stuff of a Livingstone education. Dialectical legerdemain gave new import to that age-old pedagogical cry, uttered by frustrated teachers the world over: "Pay attention." Pay attention, CAD students, you never know exactly what it is that you're being taught. Sometimes it takes decades for recalcitrant, near-delinquent, or even unusually attentive and diligent students to learn that lesson.

That is the specter, a specter entirely out of joint with apartheid's pedagogical and political intentions, that remains unaddressed in these pages but hovers—invitingly, maybe a little ominously—above this writing. This specter is nothing if not unthinkable, and this thinking runs so perversely contrary to the commonsense that was apartheid logic; it is coercive, yes, but precisely because of its heavy handedness, it is vulnerable—dare one say?—to the force of the dialectic.

The Dialectic, In Black and White

Indeed, by casting the perversity of gratitude in Adorno's terms, we come to recognize that we are a priori—as we are surely well aware—binding ourselves to the dialectic. "The unregimented thought," Adorno argues, "has an elective affinity to dialectics, which as criticism of the system recalls what would be outside the system; and the force that liberates the dialectical movement in cognition is the very same that rebels against the system. Both attitudes of consciousness are linked by criticizing one another."[12] We are bound to the dialectic in its most entangled, *dekonstructive* articulation. It is *dekonstrucive* in the sense, shared unevenly by Heidegger and Derrida, that everything is subject to being taken apart; nothing, in Derrida's rendering, is indivisible. We are bound by nothing other than the conceptual thicket that is of our own making; we are held in the thrall of the "unregimented thought." After all, how could perversity not throw all conventional wisdom, every political verity, all that is presumed to be logical (in relation to apartheid) into disarray? Such is the effect that derives from a lack of regimentation. This lack, however, should not be mistaken for the absence of intellectual discipline—au contraire. To follow the "unregimented thought" is to ascribe, willingly or not, to a series of unknown demands—a potential concatenation of demands that leads thinking down or along unfamiliar or defamiliarized paths, paths as yet unknown, paths at once and by turns alluring and replete with pitfalls, made so by the act of *alētheia*.

The dialectic binds—perversely, in this instance—because any criticism of the system that is apartheid cannot but recall that system. In so doing, we bring that system back into critical circulation ("criticism" as indefatigably circular) and, insidiously (through our *own* thinking), we restore critical life to apartheid. We thereby make, in short, that system an irrepressible force that persists, out of critical circularity, into every consecutive present. It becomes, therefore, impossible to critique apartheid without engaging in a twofold process. By taking apartheid apart, as it were, there is no choice but to, in a distinctly un–Du Boisian fashion, submit to the logic of double-consciousness—the consciousness proposed as the perversity of gratitude. By deconstructing apartheid, we bring it back into view, so that every new encounter with apartheid produced out of our double-consciousness/perversity of gratitude is, as it should be, full of potential and new insights that liberate the self and alleviate the threat of undoing the self—through, say, the return of a past trauma. If the core of Adorno's negative dialectics is to show what is lost (or in danger of being lost), then one of the effects of negative dialectics is to always remind us of the object and the concept's inadequacy. To think dialectically is to always work in the shadow of the dual negative possibility—inevitability, some might insist. As much as the object is never adequate for the concept, the concept also can never fully account for the object. In this instance, apartheid remains always to be thought once more.

Adorno's understanding of the dialectic is especially useful in that, by rejecting the positive element of the Hegelian dialectic, he makes it possible not to struggle for unity—or, fallaciously, for resolution (which, in Jameson's critique of the dialectic, is not only impossible but undesirable[13])—but to pursue what emerges out of the conflict between the two antagonistic forces. As we learn from Jameson, what Adorno's "pure" negation engenders is a thinking of the interface among concepts, objects, ideas, and the material world. We find ourselves again confronted by the recognition that the object is not equal to the concept because there can be no equivalence of that which is inherently nonidentical. If Hegel's thinking affirms identity, then Adorno's negates it by keeping object and concept distinct, refusing to weld them together, to make even a provisional One of the two. This is the condition of determinate negation, where we are reminded that there are specific contradictions between what thought claims and what it actually delivers. Once more, our thinking makes itself subject to (a further and necessary) thinking—a thinking, perhaps, of what thought must now deliver, having failed to deliver.

Nur Denken kann die Arbeit des Denkens tun.

Out of the failure of the concept or thought to deliver comes the recognition that what we take to be spontaneous experience or visceral response is a critical distrust. Experience is not that which must be negated or refused; rather, it is that which furnishes work for the concept. Experience is that which must be tested against the theoretical claims of the concept—that is, experience itself is that which must be thought, and thought to the second power, because to name experience "experience" is already the consequence of the process of thinking. Experience is already a process that has been subjected to thinking and must now be held up to the scrutiny that inheres in all theories of being.

We have just made this paradox clear. The resonant effect of Adorno's negation is that while it ascends—or is that descends?—into the realm of the positive, it nevertheless shows itself to be nothing if not generative. Out of failure comes the imperative for thinking to address that failure. The goal is not to solve the problem or to re-solve the contradiction but to confront, in all its difficulty (because of its difficulty), what now presents itself for thought for no reason other than that it is derived directly from that which was thought immediately before it and, in having been thought, suggests that there might very well be something greater to be achieved by way of negation. The dialectic is provisionally rendered as the sum of the parts that are sublated into something greater.

What pathways for thinking apartheid opens up—such pathways as apartheid itself could never have imagined. The apparent incommensurables and the articulation of a perverse gratitude explode into a raft of "negative" possibilities. The putative failure of thinking is precisely what makes thinking the only possible response to its own failure. The failure of thinking, then, not as corrective, per se, but as that which is reflexively attuned to itself. Attuned to itself *as* and *because of* failure.

After all, as Adorno is quick to note, "philosophy is more than bustle only where it runs the risk of total failure."[14] As such, to propose gratitude as a necessarily inappropriate rendering of disenfranchised apartheid education, to recall with thanks that which was intended to denigrate the disenfranchised mind and Being, is to not only risk total failure but to invite opprobrium, disbelief, and worse. The greater the philosophical risk, the higher the political stakes— especially as it risks negating a venerated oppositional (anti-apartheid) truism that by no means lacks facticity and minimizing, without going so far as to validate, the intellectual violence that was BAD, CAD, and IAD. To posit the perversity of gratitude is, unless both perversity and gratitude are made subject to thinking, to run the risk of lending succor—and possibly even an intellectual patina—to the apartheid regime's deliberate attempt to under- and miseducate generations of disenfranchised students.

In Sartre's terms, our white counterparts were the "technicians of knowledge."[15]

We were the "monsters." To extend the Sartrean analogy, perhaps to breaking point, our white contemporaries were "false" intellectuals. I would not, mischievous though I am inclined to be, be so bold as to claim that we at Livingstone were "true" intellectuals. Still, merely by raising it as a possibility, I may have already succumbed to the temptation to follow the analogy to its perverse conclusion or to its logical, not-so-perverse end. At the very least, what cannot be denied here is the disquieting effect the actions of the disenfranchised students had—an effect, as Soweto and the 1980 school boycott demonstrated, that was felt well beyond BAD, CAD, and IAD schools.[16] *Under such circumstances, we might ask that Shakespeare render Polonius perversely, so much so that Laertes and Ophelia's father* might turn from his visceral self-interest and advise, contrary to his usual predilection. Or, perhaps he could give us an equivocating Polonius radicalized by Caliban; that historical creature who undermines Polonius's sanctimony through Caliban's rude and disruptive propensities. Such a creature who offers, "Rather a 'monster' than a (white) bourgeois 'technician' be."

It may indeed be that it is only through the perverse, the intensely unnatural (Caliban), the willfully degenerate (Laertes), and the deliberately contrary (Falstaff) that it becomes possible to go "back there again." Only the perverse contains within it force enough to blow away the smog that is the commonsense of a disenfranchised apartheid education. The perverse stands in relation to thinking as a cantankerous gale-force southeaster, a wind well known to Cape Townians during winter for the havoc it whips up. Sweeping in off the Atlantic Ocean, the southeaster, also known as the Cape Doctor for clearing away the smog that covers the city, scatters umbrellas, downs power lines, uproots trees. Such is the force of a wind that blows the natural logic out of a place, leaving behind a clearing where there is space and time for thinking. The Cape Doctor is followed by a wind coming out of the northwest, the wind that brings rain. The Cape Doctor cleanses a space as if preparing the clearing for the fecundity that breeds thinking. In order to think the perversity of gratitude, it is necessary to first clear it of detritus, of debris, of anti-apartheid commonsense so that thinking might flourish. In truth, however, the clearing in which thinking takes place is of a much older vintage. It is a space cleared by a wind that first gathered its force in pre-Socratic Greece, only to find itself taken up in what would have seemed, to both Parmenides and even more so to Heidegger, who venerated the Greeks (as did Hegel), a most unlikely "there." The Dasein of Livingstone, then, constitutes, in its relationship to Parmenides, to Heidegger, its own particular perversity.

Much like the dialectic, which resolves nothing, creating instead a new knot of difficulties to be thought, the perversity of gratitude generates more, and often unexpected, strands of perversity—strands that can often be traced to thickets of impropriety, where perversity *thrives. How could perversity not thrive in these thickets, given how lushly populated they are by the flourishing unnatural and ever-multiplying degenerates, so many Calibans loosed upon the world? There are so many Calibans flying hither and tither, roaming the wide world, each determined to produce a language that can bear the weight of thinking. Impropriety is the native soil of perversity, a soil that lends itself unnaturally to the difficult work of thinking.*

Apartheid's nomenclature was not artful or subtle, but it was a powerful delimitation of the disenfranchised's "*social being*,"[17] to invoke a term from Sartre's critique of the bourgeoisie.[18] According to Sartre, the trajectory of social being is an inexorable drudgery (akin to "*destiny*"), because this "being is nothing other, in effect, than the functions they will have to fulfill day in, day out."[19] In Sartre's memorable put-down of the destiny of the middle class (especially the delimitations that mark lower middle-class life), "he is a middle man, a middling man, a middle class man."[20] And then comes the coup de grace: "The general ends to which his activities lead are not *his* ends."[21]

Apartheid had neither the linguistic facility nor the political wherewithal to produce its own Orwellian doublespeak. It certainly lacked the sharp wit and bitter irony of the Sartrean variety. In a word, its racist obviousness made clear that it lacked imagination. It may be, however, that a racism as blatant as apartheid has no need of neologisms, to say nothing of the superfluity with which it regarded wit and irony, regardless of the register in which the latter was rendered.

Instead, apartheid wrote its repressions boldly in a stark and unambiguous minimalism: "Whites Only." Apartheid operated, and not only on a rhetorical level, in white and black—pun intended. Apartheid constructed itself on the premise that it could only determine (that is, control) white South Africa's "destiny" if it overdetermined the sociopolitical being—the political fate—of the disenfranchised.

Under these conditions, it was necessary for the disenfranchised to not incessantly ponder, relentlessly contemplate, or endlessly mull over the routine humiliations and degradations that marked apartheid life. For the disenfranchised to make a life under apartheid, despite the multiple racist restrictions in place, it was necessary not to think apartheid. It became almost imperative to not, in every waking moment, think apartheid so as to not be overwhelmed by the existential violence of apartheid. Imprisoned by the military junta that ruled his native Greece in 1969, political prisoner George Mangakis acknowledges the need for respite from the ubiquity of political repression. From his tiny cell, ten feet by ten feet, Mangakis, a university professor of jurisprudence, writes movingly about the "Resistance," about solidarity, about visits to his cell by his dead brother Yannis, about his notion of "Europe" as a democratic force animated by thinking, about how prisoners sing in their moments of deepest despair (this from a man who admits to singing falsetto). For all that, Mangakis reflects, "We also need moments devoid of thought."[22]

Apartheid made me not think . . . apartheid. Only ever in moments did the need for such self-injunction present itself. Still, it may only be through those "moments devoid of thought" that it was possible to survive apartheid. It may only have been during those "moments devoid of thought" that it was possible to think apartheid.

Those moments made it possible to suspend thinking, to secure respite from thinking apartheid and from the myriad ways in which apartheid was so opposed to thinking, to live a life under apartheid where the disenfranchised self could compel itself into another mode of being while keeping safe its Being.

Is such a caring for self even possible? Is it only possible if done in a Kafkaesque fashion, meaning only if one can ignore the facticity of one's impending doom? Must one be misguided enough (or delusional in one's self-confidence) to deem oneself the equal of a system that is not only rigged but is so labyrinthine, insidious, arcane, and mendacious as to be all-consuming, threatening the self at every turn? How, then, to care for the self?

The disenfranchised had to know how—and when—to be in the world differently, from this moment to that, from this encounter (say, objecting to the belligerence of a white train conductor) to that confrontation (a run-in with a white police officer). To think or not to think, that is the question, a Shakespearean formulation of the problem that serves only to make clear the existential intensity at the core of the decision to think. To think and not to think, a question that takes second place only to Hamlet's "To be or not to be." In truth, however, these questions are co-constitutive. They belong to each other so that one would be immeasurably weakened without the other. Sometimes it is only possible to arrive at a truth through Shakespeare.

In other instances, Adorno will do as well. "Critical germs are contained," Adorno writes, "in judgment and inference, the thought forms without which not even critique of thought can do: They are never simultaneously excluding what they have failed to achieve, and whatever bears their stamp will be denied—although with questionable authority—by the truth they seek to organize."[23] Following Adorno, even if we concede apartheid as a truth that seeks to organize itself rather than as the familiar Foucauldian regime of veridiction (all the while, of course, retaining our fealty to Foucault), then it is a truth that is subject to a dialectical undoing. Though CAD sought to impose "education for barbarism," it could never insulate itself from the effects of the very regime of veridiction it intended to render as South Africa's political commonsense. Tabata's critique, its sloganistic appeal (and we should never, no matter the tendency in the slogan toward symbolic emptiness, underestimate the capacity of the slogan to rally, validate, and support political opposition in crucial moments), made of CAD's dictates a "questionable authority"—an authority drawn into question not only because of Tabata's insights (his fears for disenfranchised students, too, in truth).

During the 1980 school boycott, inflamed by the spirit of Pink Floyd's Roger Waters and David Gilmour's hit "Another Brick in the Wall," we marched around 100 Lansdowne Road singing,

We don't need no education
We don't need no thought control[24]

Pink Floyd's 1979 song proved an anthemic outlet for a polity of disenfranchised students angry at apartheid. We sang "Another Brick in the Wall" with gusto, those lines from the chorus—"We don't need no education/We don't need no thought control"—invested with particular venom at the apartheid regime as we raged against the NP's instruments of oppression. In fairness, however, we evinced the requisite solemnity in our rendering of Civil Rights standards such as "Like a Tree," and there was no shortage of reverence in our rendering of Woody Guthrie's "This Land Is Our Land." (We made the appropriate geopolitical changes to Guthrie's lyrics.) However, I have no doubt that at least a smidgen (more, in truth, maybe even much more than a smidgen) of our enthusiasm was rooted in nothing but that age-old phenomenon, teenage rebellion: "No dark sarcasm in the classroom/Teachers, leave them kids alone/Hey, teachers, leave them kids alone."[25] Nothing like good old rebellious rock 'n' roll lyrics to combine political dissent with the misanthropic energies of adolescence. Belting out "Another Brick in the Wall" during the 1980 school boycott both enveloped us in righteous anger and gave us political cover to voice our—predictable—antipathy toward our teachers. I am sure that we understood them to be, even if they were ideologically distinct from the apartheid machinery, instruments of social control. So it was certainly pleasing to engage in such obvious dissembling when we could declare, to the oppressive state and our teachers, "All in all, you're just another brick in the wall."[26] If the youth can't give voice to generational angst, what good is the revolution?

We were, then, especially passionate about instructing our teachers: "Hey, teachers, leave them kids alone." For a moment, our antipathy converged so that we could both indict the apartheid regime and let our teachers know exactly what it was we wanted from them; it was a cry for two very different—but surely equally important—forms of liberation. And, if there was going to be any "sarcasm in the classroom," we'd be the ones expressing it. Thanks to Waters and Gilmour, we could have our teenage cake and eat it too.

I doubt Adorno and his wingman Max Horkheimer would have approved of our taking up "Another Brick in the Wall" so full-throatedly in the cause of dual emancipations. Alas. Those Frankfurt School stalwarts would remain forever hamstrung by their antipathy for the popular.

It was, additionally, an "authority" made susceptible to interrogation precisely because our Livingstone teachers trained us in the art of honing "critical germs." To be anti-CAD while being held hostage by it as an educational apparatus was to, almost daily, be taught how to draw inferences—about one's place in the world as a disenfranchised student, about the kind and quality of education we were allowed to receive, about our value as human beings without fundamental rights in the land of our birth. It was also to know the importance of refining one's judgment, not the least of which was to make, again, with an insistent frequency, decisions about apartheid as a political project. In short, our capacity to judge and infer was not only fundamental to our training in thinking; it constituted those "thought forms" (which might also be designated practices) that enabled us to produce our "critiques of apartheid thought."

More to the point, the ways in which our CAD education, which was designed to exclude the disenfranchised from modernity, in all its complexity, with all its shortcomings, potentialities, and difficulties, made us think is the surest sign of what such an education failed to achieve. As disenfranchised students who made their way through the CAD and BAD syllabi, we cannot but bear the stamp of that failed denial. Through apartheid exclusion, we—anti-CAD teachers, disenfranchised students, our communities at large—found our way to organize for a truth that could sustain us. Apartheid's determination to make nothing but "barbarous" subjects of us and its propensity to enact so much violence against our bodies and our psyches served only to incline us ever more felicitously toward thinking. I. B. Tabata would surely wince at the extension of any gratitude, perverse or not, in the direction of CAD education. In truth, however, he should not. He should not because, armed with his critique, in both letter and spirit, we were better able, in our best moments, to set our sights on thinking because he helped us to understand that it was being so willfully denied us.

Under apartheid, to think or not to think was a decision that always had to be made. It had to be made at a moment's notice—a moment determined, almost invariably, by the formal apparatus of the apartheid state as well as the informal "logic" imposed by the various structures. Apartheid's logic required, on an encounter-by-encounter basis, a decision on what was, for the disenfranchised, a permissible mode of address (to a white person) and, of course, what was or could be construed as an impermissible mode of address. Such impermissibility ran the gamut of (disenfranchised behavior, perceived or real) anything from failing to use the proper honorific when speaking to a white person to refusing to behave in a sufficiently subservient way to having the temerity to disagree, in either public or private. (A white person was always to be addressed formally, as "Mr.," "Mrs.," or "Ms.," a formality that often extended, as I have written elsewhere, to white youth.)[27]

As such, the effect of apartheid governance proved to be, politically as well as culturally, a perverse Foucauldian undertaking. The disenfranchised had to be artful in discerning their response(s). They had to learn the art of dissimulation or sly civility (à la James Scott, *Weapons of the Weak*; *Domination and the Arts of Resistance*); they had to know when to turn the other cheek (all too often, in truth). In response to apartheid's unartful modes of governance, the disenfranchised had to perform the art of compliance, of being governed. No insignificant skill, that, submitting to being governed.

All encounters between the state and the disenfranchised made of the moment a potential confrontation. Because of the relative powerlessness of the disenfranchised, all such encounters were constitutively unequal, so that the moment of decision was invariably overdetermined by apartheid's discriminatory laws, legal strictures, and psychological invasiveness. The disenfranchised lived in anticipation of a series of confrontations and humiliations or, in good moments, of being the beneficiary of the kind of indifference that only (white) power can bestow upon the disenfranchised. The latter was a rare occurrence, but when it did happen, what a non-Keatsian thing white apartheid indulgence and sufferance was.

Raw state power, the indignity of obeisance, and repressed anger were among the many modes of apartheid violence made legible in the anticolonial writing of authors such as Fanon (*Black Skin, White Masks*; *The Wretched of the Earth*) and Amilcar Cabral (*Unity and Struggle: Speeches and Writings of Amilcar Cabral*) and the Black Consciousness rhetoric that pervades South African Steve Biko's work (*I Write What I Like*).

The disenfranchised must contend with warring imperatives. To think. The need to think. And not to think. To think so as to live. To know the necessity of the injunction not to think. Not to think in order to live. Not to think in order to stay alive. To procure, to secure, a life. A life under apartheid. To think or not to think, so as to make it possible to live life—to live from today until tomorrow. To live today, freed from the strictures of thinking. Or, to think today in order to be able to live—to be alive—tomorrow. To be caught between what is needed (thinking) and what is necessary (the suspension of thinking à la Mangakis, as if that were possible, in order to stay alive). To be in a world, an unimaginable one, in truth, where such distinctions could apply. "The need," according to Adorno, "is what we think from, even where we disdain wishful thinking."[28] Can the thinking of the disenfranchised be designated "wishful"? Is it wishful to wish for what is not? Does all thinking not, in one way or another, fall prey to the charge of wishfulness? Or, to follow the logic of perversity, must we not render the condition (the ideal condition?) for thinking as the need to wish for apartheid disenfranchisement? In order to think under conditions of oppression, must the subjugated not, from the beginning, surrender to wishfulness and plead guilty to such a charge?

Such is the conundrum and, dare one say, the perverse privilege of living apartheid for the disenfranchised, which begs at least these questions: Is it possible to be freed from thinking? Is that the desire that is purely wishful? Who wants to be relieved of the work of thinking? Under apartheid, who would not, at least occasionally, want to *not* think? However, isn't the decision to not think a fallacy? Does it not involve thinking so as to will the self to not think? Isn't thinking always, in such a scenario, constitutive of the impossibility of not thinking?

To "become conscious," in Kant's sense, of oneself under the conditions of apartheid, it was as necessary to think as it was to "consciously" remind oneself not to think. To come to Kantian consciousness, the disenfranchised self, under apartheid, had to learn the art of discrimination. It was necessary to enact political judgment (or to suspend judgment, one could as easily say) between those moments that demanded thinking and those occasions when the demands of everyday life, "bitter though the taste may be,"[29] as exiled South African poet Arthur Nortje phrases it, superseded the imperative to think, to think apartheid. Designated as such, to think apartheid is to recognize the force apartheid exercises on thinking while simultaneously refusing apartheid as itself constituting a thinking—that is, to know apartheid as the bare unconcealing of racism and, as such, if only for a moment, to refuse the perverse logic that allows apartheid the mental capacity to divide public life into distinct, intensely policed, racial categories. So conceived, it is possible to suggest that as much as apartheid generated (the need for) thinking, apartheid itself cannot stand as a (mode of) thinking because it is so devoid of truth. And what is thinking if not truth? Thinking is required in order to organize, both in an epistemological (categorical) and a political way, for truth, to make this commitment stand against the 'regime of veridiction,' and to expose (alētheia) the coercion of apartheid as not a logic of truth but as nothing but *raison d'Etat*.And the reason of the state, as Derrida reminds us, is nothing but the "reason of the strongest."[30]

At first glance, apartheid is disqualified from constituting (a) thinking because, as Heidegger's oeuvre so painstakingly attests, all thinking derives from the "essence of ἀλήθεια,"[31] where ἀλήθεια— alētheia—is commonly understood as truth ("truth as ἀλήθεια"[32]). In none of his other works is Heidegger so deliberate in his attention to the truth of thinking than in his lectures (on) *Parmenides*, where his fidelity to the truth of the philosophical life of Greece is most emphatic. (Critical to Heidegger's fidelity is his distaste for the Latinization of the Greeks, which for him amounts to the corruption of Greek thinking.) Heidegger, however, does not accede to ἀλήυια as "truth," although he acknowledges the resonance of this more general translation.

Instead, Heidegger renders ἀλήθεια as unconcealedness. And unconcealedness is always, for Heidegger, bound to concealedness. We must, then, approach ἀλήθεια as the inextricability of concealedness and/within unconcealedness, as well as, to phrase the matter slightly differently, the constitutive presence of unconcealedness in concealedness. We are, therefore, to think ἀλήυια as unconcealedness ↔ concealedness; ἀλήυια is the tie that binds, inextricably, the inevitable consequence of the one in the other.

Following Heidegger, then, and contra our earlier assertion, apartheid becomes eminently thinkable not as a truth but as that mode of being in the world most open to thinking because apartheid belongs so fully in the realm of ἀλήυια. This is despite apartheid's determination to keep the disenfranchised's openness to thinking in concealedness, especially if we understand "openness" in the "sense of the unconcealedness of beings."[33] The effect, then, of the "unconcealedness of beings" is that it draws all others—everything proximate to it and possibly even distant from it—into its "circle of activity" and into the essence of its being.[34] This is how the ontic exhibits—manifests—itself, an effect against which apartheid, like all other political systems, cannot immunize itself. All being is predicated upon openness toward the other because openness is always the initial sign and, to be philosophically direct, the most minimal inscription—guarantee?—of every being's being toward Being.

Apartheid is that mode of being in the world in which disenfranchised thinking can, sometimes if not always, be said to unconceal itself even as it is ostensibly—and maybe even unknowingly—presumed to be concealed. Similarly, that which conceals cannot but create the possible conditions for unconcealment. As such, apartheid stands as that unwinnable struggle waged by the forces of concealment (the apartheid regime and its various articulations in the world in which it is dominant) against unconcealment—if, that is, we grasp unconcealment as the determination of the disenfranchised to think their being in the world in order to incline more fully toward their Being in the world. It is the determination of the disenfranchised to think their being toward Being, their inclining toward a world that extends, as it must, beyond the many circumscriptions of apartheid. Again, broadly speaking, the ἀλήυια principle applies. The apartheid regime's attempts to foreclose the world to disenfranchised being could not help but fail. It must fail because the world beyond (the unconcealed), the world not subject to the dictates of apartheid (concealed), is a priori lodged within the concealedness of apartheid. To designate those variously black bodies "disenfranchised" was already an act of unconcealedness. So conceived, every act of concealedness makes itself subject to thinking, and in so doing, every thinking falls within the ambit of ἀλήυια so that—in this instance—to disenfranchise is to raise the (prospect of the) franchise into unconcealedness. Thinking is what brings the franchise into unconcealedness in the face of, and in spite of, all efforts at concealment to the contrary.

To know how to live without (temporarily) thinking must proceed through thinking (for) the (temporality of the) suppression of thought.

Disenfranchised subjects had to think in order not to think. *Puto et ne putes*. They had to think about not thinking, about how not to think, about what it would mean not to think—an insurmountable dialectic. And, in this instance, the dialectic becomes a critical weapon of the disenfranchised because, following Hegel's dictum, the "dialectic is an opponent's strength turned against him, not just in the dialectical particular, but eventually in the whole."[35] Here, we see the dialectic as jujitsu. To project the anti-CAD dialectic beyond it-self while simultaneously remaining unfailingly felicitous in relation to it: This particular "germ" that was the anti-CAD dialectic would, in February 1990, announce itself as the final act in the struggle against apartheid. It took the form of a series of small reversals, be-ginning with anti-CAD pedagogy, school boycotts, rent strikes, bus boycotts, minor acts of sabotage, and sustained moments of resis-tance that culminated in one giant overthrow of the system of apart-heid. Through the jujitsu that is dialectics, the opponent's strength is overcome—only, of course, to mark the imminent emergence of a different constellation of factors and actors in a new dialectic. But this dialectic is not so new as to render all the factors and actors unrecognizable. And so, with the renewal of the dialectic, we are reminded that "virtually all thoughts . . . cause a negative motion."[36] In every ending, there is a beginning.

From the very beginning, then, for the disenfranchised self, apartheid could only be apprehended as a perverse dialectic that demands that the disenfranchised think about what it means to be in the world as a thinking being—*corpus humanum, denkendes Sein*—who wills the self not to think.

About apartheid I can say this, declaratively: Apartheid made me think. Apartheid made me think about not thinking. Apartheid made me understand the cost—intellectual, political, socioeconom-ic—of not thinking. Apartheid revealed to me, more clearly than it ever intended, I am quite sure, how costly it could be—would be—not/to think.

What remains unarguable and is as true now as it was when I was being educated within (and, unfailingly, against) its unequal racial strictures is that in having made me think, apartheid made me—and continues to make me—grateful to it. Apartheid makes me grateful to it because it made thinking a matter of (intellectual) life and, per-haps, death. To phrase the matter as a Cartesian poetic: The end of life is not death but not thinking. *Ego puto tanto cum essen:* I am only when I think. Nothing will suffice in relation to this acknowledg-ment except to recognize a perverse gratitude to apartheid: From the very first, apartheid made thinking of the utmost importance to the life of the disenfranchised.

This is obviously not to suggest that the desire for solitude did not obtain among the disenfranchised or that such solitude was not achieved. Au contraire. The struggle for and commitment to finding, if not a Woolfian "room of one's own," at least a quiet corner in which to read was a common feature of disenfranchised life. Such a corner might have been found, say, in a library, even one that may have been decidedly under-resourced. It was still a library—that is, a building filled with books, often staffed by librarians keen to serve enthusiastic students or older patrons or to instill a love of books in younger children. Such a corner might also have been secured at home or on a crowded bus or an empty train carriage. It might simply have presented itself as an empty classroom during recess at school.

Regardless, in one form or another, this striving for solitude was almost certainly inspired by a conception of intellectual life that would have been recognizable to a figure such as Parmenides or Plato. This universal impulse toward thinking could have, in disenfranchised South Africa, just as easily been satisfied by reading in the school library or manifested itself as a mode of being (thinking) that found its voice in analyzing a Shakespearean sonnet or critiquing the NP version of South African history—the latter of which was a form of disciplinary learning that set it against the official version of South African history and was a praxis vital to the political education of most disenfranchised schoolchildren.

However, it is unarguable that the desire to achieve a life of the mind could easily have found itself thwarted by the sheer paucity of resources, by insufficient books, by the proscription of certain literatures, by a dilapidated physical plant, by poverty, by uneducated parents who saw no value in education, or by an indifferent teacher. Nonetheless, this desire for a more intense, varied, and rigorous life of the mind reminds us that there in the ranks of the disenfranchised was a mind that wanted more. After all, why would we expect it, like any other mind, to have been satisfied with what was extant? Why would we expect that the disenfranchised would limit its intellectual horizon because of apartheid? Such an expectation, articulated or not, would be truly perverse.

All of these possible intellectual encounters turn on the insistent, relentless interplay between two—shall we call them paradoxically complementary?—forces. On the one hand, there is the disenfranchised mind that lives its life in and through the public encounter with apartheid, and on the other, there is the disenfranchised mind that seeks to engage itself and the world of ideas in solitude. These divergent pulses derive from distinct ends of the political spectrum, but they are forces always at work, omnipresent and frequently roiling within the disenfranchised self. Such a struggle, which consistently asks the disenfranchised self to think in public and in private, in what can only be described as very different—but equally demanding—modes of being, recalls Du Bois's critique of the "twoness" of the Negro. "One feels ever his twoness," we remember Du Bois writing, "two souls, two thoughts, two unreconciled strivings; two warring ideals in one dark body, whose dogged strength alone keeps it from being torn asunder."[38] Du Bois is correct in his analysis, of course. It is a costly business, this dogged determination to keep body and soul together under conditions of repression, statutory discrimination, and a routine vulnerability to the oppressor's violence.

Clearly, the very act of thinking under apartheid effects division, laboring as it does under the force of the dialectic. The disenfranchised is always either split into "two souls" or on the cusp of such a violent Manicheanism. It is no small matter to hold two thoughts, especially two such diametrically opposed ones, in balance or to hold the self together even as these two thoughts pull the disenfranchised self in diametrically opposed directions. This is especially true because these "two warring ideals" are indeed at once in struggle and, as I have just argued, paradoxical in their complementarity. To think against apartheid within its sociopolitical strictures—let us name it everyday life—is as worthy an undertaking as the desire, the need, the intellectual potentiality to think in withdrawal, however difficult the work of disconnection might be.

The paradox of thinking under apartheid, then, might be that the condition for thinking seeks not to reconcile—to bring into line, to achieve a unity, shall we say, between the "two strivings" we know as public thinking and private contemplation—but to hold these strivings in tension and to activate and animate the dialectic fully. The intensification of the dialectic contains within itself the potentiality of, to invoke Arendt's "artificial world of the laboratory," bringing that which is buried within the dialectic to the surface, bringing fully into our consciousness that which we have not yet thought.[39] In Arendt's terms, this refers to that which would "not appear of its own accord" but is instead "forced to appear and to disclose itself."[40] What is being demanded of the disenfranchised self is to make of irreconcilability an onerous condition, to make of it, as Du Bois is well aware, a political and intellectual virtue.

In this thinking for irreconcilability, the disenfranchised self seeks to force a thinking out of the dialectic that is not at first, or perhaps even at all, visible; it seeks to make a new thinking appear, but only in part, out of "its own accord." The perversity of such a thinking of apartheid is that it does not know, because it can never know in advance (it is entirely clueless) exactly what might be disclosed. Thinking dialectically, then, thinking through the experience of the irreconcilable rises to the level of the event. To resist apartheid by thinking apartheid as an irreconcilability is to encounter apartheid as that condition that makes the disenfranchised self indebted to that mode of thinking that only apartheid, perversely and at considerable cost, could make possible: The event of thinking—thinking as the only act that can stand, under apartheid, as the event. Such is the perversity of gratitude.

Interlude III

In-Gratitude

In "Racism's Last Word," Jacques Derrida offers a prospect in his critique of apartheid that is temporal, as befits the logic of the event. Derrida's temporality, it could be argued, is prospective in that it anticipates what might be.[1] It looks forward to another moment, one that is not yet but that lies, with the promise of prospect, already embedded in *l'avenir*— what is to come. It lies in a moment that is ours if we grant to that *l'avenir* a trajectory that arches back to, say, February 1990 or, if you insist, to April 1994. Of apartheid, Derrida writes, "For its movement does not yet belong to any time or space that might be measured today. Its course rushes headlong, it commemorates in anticipation: not the event but the one it calls forth."[2]

Derrida's "today," then, belongs to our day, to that movement in history that has encoded itself in our time and space. What Derrida sought in 1984 to anticipate we now find ourselves in a position to commemorate—at the time of writing, South Africa, almost thirty years after the country's first democratic elections. That event is ours to commemorate, to speak of, to speak in the name of, to speak as though it had yielded something, to speak as though history has been, as it were, productive.[3]

It is, however, precisely such a capacity to speak—commemoratively or not—that seems to me now an impossibility. Derrida notes: "For such here is the *invention* and the oeuvre of which it is here fitting to speak: South Africa *beyond* apartheid, South Africa in memory of *apartheid*."[4] This is what the event is meant to call forth: "South Africa beyond apartheid," South Africa in which apartheid is a memory but never, one imagines, memorialized.

However, in expressing the titular perversity of gratitude, this writing a priori orients us differently. Specifically, it points us in the direction that seeks to recover and give voice to a living memory of apartheid—that is, a thinking that declares itself (perversely, again) grateful to apartheid, to an apartheid education. *The Perversity of Gratitude*, then, seeks not to dispose of or dispense with the memory of apartheid but to instead "speak"—in Derrida's spirit—the life, the mode of intellectual life that apartheid made possible.

To speak to what it calls forth is to speak perversely of apartheid—all the while, of course, implicitly refusing to consider such an expression of gratitude anything but perverse. This intellectual debt is thought as not perverse but historic. The debt of gratitude arises from the recognition that this type of thinking emerged out of thinking against apartheid as singular; this is the kind of thinking only apartheid could have made possible. The event named "thinking" calls us forth, revealing that what is lodged at the core of every unthought—educational systems carved out of what the regime imagined to be that which was most likely not to produce thinking—is a radical kernel of thinking (to invoke again Žižek's work on St. Paul). The mark of a thinker's profundity and fecundity, according to Heidegger, is the reservoir (the depth and capacity) of his unthought; the greater the unthought, the more there is to a thinker's thinking. To cast Heidegger's contention in Adorno's terms, "Represented in the inmost cell of thought is that which is unlike thought."[5]

At first glance, Adorno would appear to—accustomed as we are to only expecting the negative (dialectic) from him—negate Heidegger's proposal. However, Adorno's declarative stands as a negation only if we fail to apply the logic of the contradiction to his pronouncement. Contradiction, in Adorno's terms, is not only that which negates. The contradiction is also that mode of thinking that allows the particular to emerge—as fully as possible—into its particularity. Let us, then, allow the particularity of disenfranchised apartheid education to come into its own. More than that, let us allow it to flourish within the context of *Negative Dialectics*. If, at the very core, at the epicenter that was disenfranchised apartheid education, was that which was most "unlike thought," then disenfranchised apartheid education was almost the most well-adapted historical and political organism in which thinking could flourish. The germ of all anti-apartheid thinking resided within apartheid thinking—in all apartheid thinking, in every one of its institutions, in all of its structures, in every one of its political bureaucracies.

Understood as such, there is nothing to do but reveal that the structural unthought that apartheid education was intended to be instead proved itself to be the perfect negative foil—the first axis of the contradiction—through which thinking (let us figure it as anti-apartheid thinking) could be taught as well as learned. This perverse gratitude is, it must be acknowledged, a thinking—thanking, *danke, denke*, as we know Heidegger insists upon their common etymologies—that can only be called forth outside of apartheid. *Outside* here means after the time of apartheid, so that what apartheid calls forth is, in strictly temporal terms, postapartheid; it means being outside the geopolitical space but never being devoid of the anti-apartheid ethos in which apartheid was encountered—that is, lived as an everyday experience.

Punning on South Africa's colonial importance (and, in the process, evoking the city in which I lived apartheid, Cape Town), Derrida follows his thinking on the "beyond" and "memory" of apartheid with, "Such would be the heading and the cape to be rounded, yet everything will have begun in exile."[6] Derrida offers a political direction, a democratic vista that can be sighted once the cape has been rounded: The promise of the direction in which his act of writing is headed, the direction in which it wants to direct us; that is where we should be headed. Derrida's reference to "exile," of course, refers to the "'works of art,' signed 'creations'"[7] that form part of the exhibition on which he is commenting.

If, we might argue, apartheid's transgressions acquire a special resonance from within that condition we know as exile, then there is something historically appropriate, and therefore by no means unexpected, about articulating a perverse gratitude to apartheid from that self-same locale. There is, as Derrida explains, a particularity to deracination that accounts for the different ways in which—in this case—the historically disenfranchised respond to their removal from the place of origin. "All expatriates," Derrida writes, "remain singular."[8] Exile, then, is anything but a uniform experience in which declamation of the place of origin issues from every quarter of the diaspora. Or, to render the diaspora as an experience that is inherently complicated, palimpsest, and even given to ostensibly unsustainable contradictions, it is only because of such a singularity that apartheid can be condemned by the exile/d and thought against the prevailing political ethos. Exile may very well be that locale from where condemnation issues as the first articulation of remove. However, the exiled, in thinking their exile, are by no means assured of having the last word.

It is necessary to pause for a moment to maintain clarity, as this act of thanking involves a struggle with contradictions. To express a historic and public debt of gratitude to apartheid education is to recognize the desire to stop short of thanking apartheid and yet to know the very perversity of that proximity to such an expression. It is to acknowledge the pervasiveness of the thank-you and to understand that the linguistic form that gratitude assumes most often in our daily lives, in our everyday exchanges, is precisely that phrase: "Thank you."[9] How is it possible to be grateful for having been legally condemned to receive an inferior education? How can one even imagine saying "thank you" for having been compelled to attend schools that were, as a matter of political decision, deliberately under-resourced? The schools the disenfranchised had no choice but to attend were marked by too few facilities, and the teachers' capacity was stretched by the number of their pupils and the quality of the apparatus at hand. Apartheid education was specifically conceived so as to ensure that an absolute minimum of disenfranchised pupils matriculated[10] from high school.

Writing from Beyond

It is very likely that this perverse thinking of gratitude could only have begun in exile. We might name it the condition of living outside

("Here"—the Unites States, from where I write) while remaining forever, in one articulation or another, tethered to a constitutively different, removed inside ("There"—the apartheid past, to and of which I write). Neither description seems sufficient because the diaspora, for all its similarities to living "in exile," is not commensurate with the latter. The exile has, in almost all cases, no choice. Living in the diaspora is the consequence of a political decision. "There" has become, for a whole series of reasons, explicable as well as inarticulable, unlivable. "There" cannot sustain life in way that "Here" can. "There," of course, and this is the crux of the matter, can be abandoned but will not be left behind. Every "Here" bears the ineradicable inscription of the abandoned "There."

However, the act of writing from beyond is to recognize that the choice—a decision that is vexed and, as such, a choice that understands its own constitutive lack of agency (it will, as such, never amount to a "free choice")—to relocate to "Here" is always an a priori one. The decision to leave "There" is always made (most often a long time) before the actual physical act of departure. The self has left before it departs. Departure, as such, is what follows leaving, follows the decision to leave. Writing from beyond, writing from "Here," is nothing other than enacting the decision (after Kierkegaard, we know that the decision changes everything) to not return while remaining forever umbilically linked to "There" while trying, again and again, always unsuccessfully, to shuck off the unbreakable ties that bind the self to "There."

Writing from beyond, then, makes it possible to say that a work such as this was produced—thought—in exile only if the exilic permits of the impossibility of leaving. It is possible to depart from "There," but "There" can, as it were, never be left in any psychopolitical sense. The self is always irrefutably, against its will, "There"—even, or most especially, when it is "Here." There can be, under the condition of writing from beyond, no certainty of place. The self, under this condition, is at once neither "Here" nor "There," in moments both "Here" and "There," and also by turns "Here" and "There." In Derrida's phrasing, "As if from now we didn't dwell there any longer, and to tell the truth, as if we had never been at home."[11]

Writing from beyond might then be, as Derrida understands it, that writing that emanates from the violence that is the geography of birth.

It is a *dis*location—"as if we had never been at home." While this is indictment enough, it is still insufficient to fully explicate what it means to write from beyond. Writing from beyond is simultaneously an affirmation of the tyranny of the geopolitical (the self can never escape the geopolitical stamp issued and inscribed upon it at birth)—the ineradicable (that which will not be excised) sovereignty of the geopolitical—and the marking(s) of a striving toward resisting the geography of birth that knows (even in its not knowing), a priori, the tremendous force of the geopolitical.

Derrida is poetic about this state of the self, pronouncing that "what resists analysis also calls for thinking otherwise."[12] As such, writing from beyond registers itself as a "thinking otherwise." More than that, however, writing from beyond speaks the absolute violence that constitutes the dialectic out of which the interplay, the brutal relation between "There" and "Here," is constituted. This is where we must extend Derrida by positing that it is not "as if we had never been at home"; instead, the very possibility of "home" as such was, before leaving and well before departure, never a possibility. Writing from beyond is writing against the possibility of a home. Writing from beyond is writing in the recognition of the possibility of a home. And, finally, in an act of tragic resistance, writing from beyond is such a writing that only the geopolitical, the domestic and national impossibility of home, can produce. Writing from beyond is the writing available only to those who could not even propose the conditional "as if."

Writing from beyond is writing that owes itself to the preclusion of the conditional. It is, within the paradigm that is the perversity of gratitude (as concept, conceptually speaking), to write toward an articulation that can bear the apartheid-imposed weight of "home" as an impossibility. It is, in this way, to register and to reflect the value and political import of not being able to be "at home." Writing from beyond is that writing that serves as a record of (invoking Derrida) the fecundity of the "remainder"—the "cinders and ashes" of what was and what will always be. It is what flows from the recognition that "context is never annulled without remainder."[13] As such, writing from beyond is an expression of gratitude to the inability of the context to remain within itself. The perversity of gratitude renders every context, regardless of how much or how little it is able to impose itself upon the life of the polis, infelicitous to itself.

The context is made susceptible to critique not because of itself but because its sovereignty over itself is, first and last, fictional. The context, as it understands itself, is precisely that element of the context that escapes the context. As such, the fecundity of the remainder opens the context as and beyond itself. It opens the context to itself in moments and modes that would take the context itself by surprise; it exposes the context to modes unknown to itself.

As such, writing from beyond is so perforce resistant to analysis that there is nothing to do but call for a "thinking otherwise." The perversity of gratitude is a project of retrieval from the irredeemable that does not know it is a retrieval project and is unwilling to let the irredeemable be in itself; the perversity of gratitude will not allow the irredeemable to be by itself. In the process, what the perversity of gratitude achieves—if such a term might be permitted—is to make the irredeemable (apartheid in general, its educational apparatus especially) unrecognizable both to itself and to those whom the irredeemable acted against with violence and the kind of indifference and unrestricted authority of which (a) only power such as apartheid is capable (a power unchecked, and certainly not subject to being held in check by those whom it subjugates).

Sans Faute

> I will still be caught in the circle of debt and restitution with which the nonnegotiable will have to be negotiated. I will be struggling, interminably, forever, and even before having known it, up the point, perhaps, when I would affirm the absolute anachronic dissymmetry of a debt without a loan, acknowledgement or possible restitution.
>
> —Derrida, "At This Very Moment in This Work Here I Am"

All expressions of gratitude must run the risk of fault. Phrased categorically, there is fault to be found in all expressions of gratitude. For my part, I cannot write about perverse gratitude *sans faute*. Writing faultlessly is, of course, precluded from the very beginning because it presumes a political innocence that is unattainable. In his critique of Descartes's *Cogito, ergo sum*, Emmanuel Levinas reflects on the violence of responsibility to the other. "It is," Levinas writes, "a being torn up from oneself for another in the giving to the other of the bread out of one's mouth.... The identity of the subject is here brought out, not by a rest on itself, but by a restlessness that drives me outside of the nucleus of my substantiality."[14] The violence of the phrase "a being torn up from oneself" is followed by a distinctly Christian image—to give "to the other of the bread out of one's mouth"—culminating in the act of deracination that hints at the self-induced, a "restlessness that drives me outside of the nucleus of my substantiality." In order: The self, at risk; the self assuming responsibility for the alimentary needs of the other (recalling Jesus-the-Christ feeding the multitude—the parable of the loaves and the fishes); the self putting the self (itself) at risk because of a "restlessness" that arises from within.

Thinking responsibility for (and to) the other is the hallmark of Levinas's oeuvre. However, in what way would this responsibility figure in *The Perversity of Gratitude*? After all, under apartheid, it was the disenfranchised self who was on the receiving end of the violence. How does that self now locate itself in relation to the apartheid other who perpetrated violence against the disenfranchised self within the classroom, that other who sought to condemn the disenfranchised pupil to become a "hewer of wood and a drawer of water" (Joshua 9:21)? Would that historic disenfranchised self not now be committing a retrospective violence against itself by offering gratitude to that other? Would the disenfranchised self not diminish its anti-apartheid "substantiality" through this expression of gratitude?

Inquiries, uncertainties, and protestations, imbued with a political logic and resonant as they may be with an ethical sensibility, reveal themselves as consonant with a narrative that dominated anti-apartheid and continue to exercise a hold on postapartheid conceptions of the effects of apartheid education for the disenfranchised. In his delineation of responsibility to the self, which girds his critique but rarely achieves prominence for itself, Levinas disrupts—if not entirely, then certainly "substantively"—the prevailing discourse. It is through perversity, and possibly only through perversity, that it becomes possible to discern the thinking that was, before itself, always—publicly, not as a form of sly civility—and already located at the very core of disenfranchised education. What the conceptual perversity of gratitude reveals, what is "brought out," in Levinas's terms, is the "identity of the subject" that was perpetually (in the classroom and out—out of the classroom because of what took place within the confines of the disenfranchised school) restive. As Levinas would have it, this was a "subject" who was not allowed to "rest." The disenfranchised subject was not allowed to rest on its laurels, a posture in relation to learning that was in and of itself impermissible at an institution such as Livingstone.

Levinas's thought comes to us awkwardly in translation ("not by a rest on itself"), but the unfamiliarity of the turn of phrase cannot diminish the point that is being driven toward. In order to articulate and understand the thinking that (in-)formed anti-apartheid education and arrive at the "identity" of that historical subject, something disruptive must be done. In order to bring out that identity, it is necessary to violently— without any sympathy for the travails, injustices, and injuries that this subject endured and its demands, with absolute justification, for its own narration—dislodge that subject from itself.

However, to admit of a restlessness, to say nothing of the restiveness that marked the institutional life of disenfranchised students from 1975 onward (which, as we know, gave rise to the event that was Soweto 1976), is already to acknowledge that something of (political, intellectual) substance was constitutively at work in the anti-apartheid pupil's life and in their thinking. At work is a restlessness that extradites the self from its very core; this restlessness (and the force with which it was operative) is what we can now say expelled the disenfranchised self from itself and threatens to undo the very substantiality of that self. It promises, we might even say, to disarticulate that self from itself, and in so doing, it commits not a violence against that self but performs an excavation and archivization of self, that which constitutes the self in its truth, that rises to the level of thinking.

An Apartheid Miseducation

I want to become conscious of myself only as thinking.

—**Immanuel Kant**, *Critique of Pure Reason*

This is a complex and unstable knot which I try to untangle
by recognizing the threads common to Nazism and anti-
Nazism, the law of resemblance, the inevitability of
perversion.

—**Jacques Derrida**, "Heidegger, the Philosophers' Hell"

The temptation to succumb to the lure of the declarative is great, and so
I shall, no matter that the declarative is easily and justifiably mistaken
for hubris in this instance.

I *only* think because of apartheid. That I think puts me in the debt
of apartheid. The *logos* (the logic, the word) of this gratitude, the gratitude which I so clearly just expressed, is revealing. It shows, if we follow
Derrida's critique of Heidegger, the "inevitability of perversion." But how
could perversion possibly be inevitable? Because when one thing (Nazism) shares a common thread with another thing (anti-Nazism) that is
its polar opposite, when this one thing is entangled with that one thing,
then the "law of resemblance" emerges. The effect of this law, under the
best circumstances, is to shock us out of our dialectical complacency, locating us firmly within Derrida's "complex and unstable knot." That the
entanglement is complex we grant without so much as a murmur. That
the knot is unstable, however, poses a particular threat, exposing an even
more dangerous thread—that thread which leads to thinking. Should
we pull at the wrong thread or pull too hard on it, we could do ourselves
irreparable harm. We could undo ourselves entirely. Perversity, if you are
not careful, could kill you.

Derrida, the Sephardic Jew, risks this harm in his determination to
think Heidegger, the German Nazi sympathizer who could never acknowledge his complicity with National Socialism.

Heeding the siren's call that is thinking, *The Perversity of Gratitude*
follows suit; it follows the example set by thinking.

To put your life in the hands of your thinking. To risk your life by thinking.

A triangle comes into view: There is the Algerian-born French philosopher and the historically disenfranchised South African, each in their various register drawing deeply on the German philosopher's thinking.

This is how things should be, whatever the philosophical asymmetries, ideological disparities, and levels of perversity in play. It turns out that I came to know my perverse gratitude to apartheid through Heidegger—through Derrida too, but Heidegger above all. *Martin Heidegger Saved My Life*. He saves it still today and might again tomorrow and the day after. The debts accumulate—debts of a dubious provenance, debts that have made possible an inclining toward thinking, a singular intellectual joy.

These are the threads of symmetry: Apartheid; Heidegger; a racist regime; a Nazi sympathizer. This is one face of the "law of resemblance." Such a law was made to revel in perversion, to think through perversion, to think because of perversion.

The disenfranchised came to thinking through a racist structure that did everything in its power (and it was a considerable power) to occlude and prevent disenfranchised thinking. There are common threads indeed, but they are of a perverse genus.

Out of the perversity of gratitude emerges a hard truth that is unpalatable to some and no doubt intolerable to others. It is an offense to many more besides, but it is a truth nonetheless, one that can come into itself only through thinking. It is a truth that begins with this truth. Apartheid constituted the optimal conditions for thinking. Truer still, apartheid provided the optimal conditions under which the disenfranchised were provoked to thinking. Through disenfranchising the majority of the population, apartheid made it, more than anything else, absolutely necessary for the disenfranchised to think. For the disenfranchised to live under apartheid, it was necessary to think—to think apartheid, to think against apartheid, to think, in either a politically committed or even simply a fanciful way, a world beyond apartheid. To invoke Hamlet in a spirit entirely contrary to the tenor of that famous soliloquy, "perchance to dream, ay there's the rub."[15] Instead of Hamlet's suicidal contemplations, the determination to dream another world. Apartheid made imperative, perversely, a thinking that could only emerge from within the strictures of apartheid, a thinking indebted entirely to the restrictions imposed by apartheid. It is a perverse thinking that bears the hallmark of the immersive dialectics proposed by Adorno, as we have by now intuited, in his signature work, *Negative Dialectics.*

"At a distance," Adorno writes, "dialectics might be characterized as the elevation to self-consciousness of the effort to be saturated with dialectics."[16] Following Adorno's theory of "dialectical saturation," it is possible to argue that thinking the apartheid/anti-apartheid dialectic can only come into its own—can only achieve "self-consciousness," come into its truth, as it were—because of a volatility inherent to dialectical thinking. To be educated as a disenfranchised subject within (and by) the apartheid system was to be a priori in possession of a dialectical consciousness—a consciousness in struggle with itself because it is a consciousness in struggle with its simultaneous location within the apartheid educational apparatus while being opposed to this self-same system.

Dialectics, as Adorno understands it, is always at war with itself so that it is constantly on the verge of undoing itself because of the untruth in which it is saturated. It is for this reason that "the free part of thought ... represents the authority which already knows about the emphatic untruth of that real-systematic context. Without this knowledge, there would be no eruption; without adopting the power of the system, the outbreak would fail."[17] It is precisely this "free part of thought," that thinking which (repeatedly, on a day-to-day basis) grasped and resisted the political inequity of the "real-systematic context," that formed the bedrock of disenfranchised opposition to apartheid. It is this knowledge that gave rise to the many instances of anti-apartheid eruptions, from labor strikes to school boycotts, from violent protests to mournful marches.

Concepts 4

Withdrawal

Disenfranchised apartheid education so conceived, then, would not allow the luxury of thinking in or through withdrawal, a conception of what it means to think that has long plagued philosophical approaches to this question. However, this does not mean that withdrawal did not figure in or inform disenfranchised thinking. Nevertheless, the first imperative was urgency and the racist immanence of apartheid. Because of this, to think under apartheid, to think because of or despite apartheid, was to think being in the world; it was to, in Hannah Arendt's critique of Descartes and Plato, live the impossibility of withdrawal from the world. Taking up a quote from Descartes, Arendt delineates (and rejects, in her larger argument) the most conventional understanding of thinking:

> Withdrawal from the "beastliness of the multitude" into the company of the "very few" but also the absolute solitude of the One has been the most outstanding feature of the philosopher's life ever since Parmenides and Plato discovered that for those "very few," the sophoi, the "life of thinking"

that knows neither joy nor grief is the most divine of all, and *nous*, thought itself, is "the king of heaven and earth."[1]

In truth, to live as a disenfranchised self under apartheid was to know life as the "beastliness of the multitude." It was to live as an undifferentiated, unindividuated self whose most defining sociopolitical feature was that self's racial identity. In order to aspire, even at the most rudimentary level, to the condition of the philosophical One, it was imperative to first think apartheid and its constraints—and, of course, to understand those constraints as, perversely, the first motor of thought.

III

Stanley Gordon Moysey Ridge

Thespian from Natal

There is no experience which is not a way of thinking.

—Michel Foucault, *The History of Sexuality, Volume 2*

The world is inexhaustible but offers itself only in
specificity and in manifold gradations of the kinds of
existence.

—Rüdiger Safranski, *Martin Heidegger:*
Between Good and Evil.

When I enrolled in UWC in January 1981, I was entering a tertiary institution set aside mainly for those the apartheid regime designated coloureds. As such, it fell under the jurisdiction of CAD.

I would quickly come to know and benefit immensely from an English Department faculty dedicated to teaching, despite the fact that UWC
was widely regarded by outsiders, and some within its halls, pejoratively.
In the South African colloquial, UWC was referred to as a "Bush College," a second- or even a third-rate institution designed by the apartheid
regime to educate coloureds for "barbarism"—a barbarism of a higher
order than Tabata might have imagined, but a barbarism nonetheless.

Among its students and the community in general, the university was
often referred to simply as "Bush." Many at my old high school would
not have deigned to attend Bush. Most of my Livingstone teachers were
UCT graduates. Most of my teachers would not have deigned to have
their own children apply to UWC, let alone darken its halls.

As a working-class student with a less than stellar academic record, I had no choice, and for that I remain grateful, because, as Foucault points out, "the games of truth and error through which being is historically constructed as experience; that is, as something that can and must be thought."[1] At least as much as Livingstone, UWC made me think. In the process of being made to think—to think anew, to think in a different (ideological) register—I was exposed to an experience, as Safranski would have it, that was manifold in its gradations, revealing to me the kind of existence that had the great benefit of throwing into question the intellectual ways (ideologies, predispositions) in which Livingstone had trained me. As such, UWC by no means constituted an inexhaustible world, but as an institution of tertiary learning, it stood in sharp contrast to the political verities and Trotskyist tenor of Livingstone. Though not quite the dialectic, the two institutions' specificities were just antithetical enough to make me recognize that Livingstone's ideological inclinings was incommensurable with that of UWC. The swift transition from high school to university demanded that I think both institutions in their specificity and, in so doing, make yet one more inventory of the class distinctions that obtained within the ranks of the disenfranchised. In short, if UWC was not Livingstone, I was now called on to account for the differences between the two and to understand how these institutions stood in relation to each other in my intellectual trajectory.

Livingstone faced west when the matter of tertiary education arose. Livingstone looked to the lower slopes of Table Mountain, where UCT sat, imperiously perched, looking out over the expanse of the Cape Peninsula. From its lofty locale, you can cast your gaze east to west, from the Indian Ocean to the Atlantic. On a clear day, the distant Hottentot's Holland Mountain can be spotted. UWC, however, cannot be sighted. During apartheid, UCT stood proudly as the bastion of white, Anglo, liberal privilege. South Africa's oldest university and Africa's finest, by most accounts, UCT was renowned as a teaching and research institution. Founded in 1829, UCT traced its origins to that moment when British imperialism was ascendant. Appropriately, Cecil John Rhodes was among its most generous benefactors. UCT, in other words, long preceded apartheid and, as such, could be affected but never stained by the

NP regime—at least, that's how it acted. To its mind, UCT was, both literally and figuratively, above such machinations.

Livingstone graduates who headed for the lower slopes of Table Mountain to further their education inherited no small amount of that snobbery. UWC was again literally beneath them—and beyond them too, at least insofar as it did not appear on their educational radar. What is more, UWC, unlike UCT, was an English-medium institution. UWC, brought into being under the rule of the Afrikaner regime, was technically a "dual-medium" institution, meaning that half of every lecture had to be in one of the two official languages, English and Afrikaans. So I received half of my history class in Afrikaans, half of my private law class in Afrikaans. It was quite something to hear our constitutional law class, taught by Mr. Devenish, a native English speaker possessing only the barest rudiments of Afrikaans, fight his way through the Afrikaans half of the class.

Like UCT, Livingstone was an English-medium institution, at least in the senior classes (standards 9 and 10). There was one Afrikaans-medium class up to standard 8, after which they were phased out. At the end of standard 8, Livingstone's Afrikaans-medium students were left with no choice—unless they acquired a sudden proficiency in English[2]—but to transfer to an Afrikaans-medium high school or at least one that offered a dual-medium option.[3] There can be no argument that native Afrikaans speakers formed a minority at Livingstone and were hardly held in the same regard as their English counterparts. Here, Foucault rings true—"There is no experience which is not a way of thinking"—because it unconceals the ways in which my Livingstone education, for all its accomplishments, for all its bequests, was not, despite its best efforts, always an equal experience for all.

The experience of Livingstone's Afrikaans-speaking students (their specificity) makes clear that the institution left much to be desired (courtesy of the hegemony of English), in no small measure because their experience shed an unflattering light upon our—and here I include all of the institution's English-speaking majority—way of thinking. Some of our antipathy to Afrikaans as a language derived, with good political reason, from the fact that it was the language of the apartheid regime. Thus,

Foucault would say, our "thought had a historicity that was proper to it."[4] Our colleagues in 7A, however, could not have been further removed from the regime. After all, they were exactly like us, except that we spoke the institution's lingua franca. And that difference is all the difference there is. What truths and veridictions a language bears, all at once, in harmony, in the sharpest conflict. Again, in Safranski's terms, the "world" of Livingstone is best understood in terms of how it "offered itself" in its specificity; how it revealed its "manifold gradations of existence" and the difficulty that resided in each and every gradation.

Against the backdrop of this conundrum, Heidegger once more announces himself. More to the point, he makes his thinking pertinent. What is "philosophically primary," he writes, "is not a theory of concept-formulation in historiology, nor the theory of historical knowledge, nor even the theory of history as the object of historiology; what is primary is rather the interpretation of genuinely historical beings with regard to their historicality."[5] As "genuinely historical beings" interpreted now "with regard to their historicality," what is brought into unconcealment is more than simply—which is, of course, by no means a simple matter, so the turn of phrase is idiomatic but misleading—the peripheral status of generations of 7As at Livingstone. It is also the case that 7Fs are "genuinely historical beings," but what was presented to them—us—was an entirely different cluster of interpretations to be thought. The 7Fs collectivity exceeded, by some considerable measure, in terms of generational standing, raw numbers and the governing ethos of the 7As. Even with so insistently and proudly anti-apartheid a milieu as Livingstone,[6] historical beings differed in their historicality. Relations to the institution were not only mediated, they were overdetermined by language. What is more, the effect of language nativity, if such a term might be permitted, could not be contained by the institution. Its effects rippled, bidirectionally. They rippled in ever-smaller concentric circles toward 100 Lansdowne Road and, more traumatically, in ever-growing concentric circles out from Livingstone, outward to those reaches where Livingstone's very cachet, its status and its history, functioned dialectically. And the dialectical reveals its full complexity only when apprehended in its specificity, only when the "manifold gradations of existence" are brought into presence by its having been thought.

On the one hand, to be a working-class Livingstone student was to know the self as being marked by alienation from one's own working-class community. It was to be alienated from those working-class environs because the student was thoroughly saturated with the school's ethos. On the other hand, in terms that derive entirely from language and the hierarchy it embodied, to be immersed in the Livingstone milieu marked nothing so much as privilege in a whole host of registers made intimate to us in Richard Hoggart's *The Uses of Literacy*.

To speak English was a privilege that gained the student access to Livingstone in a neighborhood where there was no equivalent—that is, a community that could not boast of such a storied, venerated, esteemed—institution. This mode of "being," as Heidegger puts it, "can show itself in its own terms."[7] What Heidegger offers as unconcealment bites here with the sharp edge of (self)indictment, as perhaps it should. At the very least, it makes of privilege, no matter how relative, what it makes of the perversity of gratitude, a matter naturally inclined toward the dialectic.

Contra Livingstone's motto, *Nulla vestige retrosum*, it was sometimes wise, if only for the sake of self-preservation, to take a step or two back from the institution. In so doing, this being also shows itself in its own terms. A dialectical engagement is necessary if the terms of this being are to be properly approached and critically apprehended. Such is the difficulty of Being, as evinced through being. The question of Being is a persistent presence made urgent by how it resides in all modalities of being.

Through these engagements and confrontations with the dialectic, we come, as Heidegger knows, to know the "fundamental constitution of the everydayness of Da-sein."[8] The question that first gave us pause remains stubbornly with us, striated now by a range of experiences only invoked earlier on. How vexed was the being of any and all Livingstone students' "Da-sein." How remarkable and challenging was the "everydayness" of this student's pedagogical life. The fundamental constitution of Da-sein unconceals itself in the mere appellation "A" as opposed to "F." (The specificity of the Livingstone class designation system was the transparency of the relationship it named between alphabetical letter and academic expectation, at least in the senior grades. Students in 9 and 10 A and B were, for the most part, expected to pursue professions in medicine, law, teaching; students in 10 C or D were not. Having passed through that system, I recall that the distinctions seemed clear to me then, perhaps clearer than now, more than forty years later, when those designations carry so much less weight.)

It is only through this everydayness that the many facets of the phenomenon—which derives from *phantesthai*—that is Livingstone "shows itself."[9] Expanding upon his delineation on the phenomenon, Heidegger offers "*phainomenon agathon* . . . a good that looks like—but in reality is not what it gives itself to be," so that it becomes possible to distinguish between *phainomenon* as "self-showing and 'phenomenon' as 'semblance.'"[10]

However, it must be remembered that what distinguishes "A" from "F" is by no means the sum total of the Livingstone experience. Heidegger's understanding of "phenomenon" in no way undermines that experience. Instead, it serves to concatenate a committed anti-apartheid pedagogy to language and class. This difficult alignment of political forces makes for a heady cocktail possessed of entanglements that are nothing if not, for a Livingstone alumnus of that era, an invitation. The cocktail is that which is redolent with the "*Parousia* or *ousia*—'presence'" of thought.[11] It is ripe for thinking and is made ripe for thinking by decades of having been marinated in a thinking that was always threatening to articulate itself into *Parousia*—as well it should have.

As Heidegger renders it in his critique of Kant, "self-showing . . . [is] the emanation of something that makes itself known but *conceals* in its appearance."[12] As such, what the event of Livingstone conceals is by no means as substantive as what it unconceals, but what it conceals is nevertheless in need of unmasking. The ontology of an institution such as Livingstone is always to be found in the interplay between concealment and unconcealment, between self-showing and self-non-showing/self-withholding. It is for this reason that, as Heidegger declares, "*Ontology is only possible as phenomenology.*"[13]

To render the matter analogically, the Afrikaans-speaking boys composed the bulk of Livingstone's rugby teams—rough, tough lads thriving in a high-contact sport they loved. They would show us English speakers, little ponces that we were, a thing or two, especially in the scrum or when a ruck and maul developed. They whipped us in our interclass games by an embarrassing margin. I can still remember the delight they took in their victory. We English-speaking lads played football. There we reigned. But our margin of victory in no way emulated theirs.

There is an old Oxbridge truism about the (class) difference between rugby and football. Rugby is said to be a game for hooligans played by gentlemen. Football, on the other hand, is a game for gentlemen played by hooligans. I could not, in my Livingstone days (nor can I now), distinguish the gentlemen from the hooligans. I can only recall the physical beating we English-speaking boys took in 1977 when my class, 7F, was laid to waste by our Afrikaans-speaking counterparts in 7A. As Muhammad Ali would have said, they "whupped us." And what is worse, their classroom was right next to ours, at the school's southern edge, so there was no escaping the specter of our defeat. (In 1977, 7A and 7F were assigned classrooms in a building known as "The Stables," as horses had, so the story went, once been quartered there.)

The class designation system, pun only partly intended because it is only partly appropriate, at Livingstone was organized in ascending order. (The pun is only partly appropriate because, broadly speaking, there was no sustainable socioeconomic distinction between language groups; still, the difference in cultural capital between the hegemonic Livingstone majority and the Afrikaans-speaking minority was substantial.) The Afrikaans-speaking class was, in this schema, at the bottom of the totem pole. "A" only conveniently coincided with their first language, Afrikaans. The difference between 7A, on the one hand, and 7F or 7G, on the other, was, if not exactly measurable, palpable. Salient is that in the senior years, standards 9 and 10, the system reverted to type; 9A and 9B were at the top of the pecking order.

It is no wonder that 7A wanted to subject us to, as the French say, an *être trop fort* on the rugby field. We had it coming.

I have no doubt that I was, if only viscerally, more attuned to this hierarchy because when I left Livingstone at 3:00 P.M., I returned to my working-class community (Hanover Park), where Afrikaans, and then certainly not a formal brand of the language, was the lingua franca. In my neighborhood, people spoke what can only be described as patois, a basic Afrikaans peppered with English phrases and, yes, "street talk." Among my friends in Hanover Park, as a native English speaker, I was a minority. It was because of my class alienation, then, mediated and modulated by language preference and facility, that, much like 7A's rugby players, I knew the condition of being outside. Their relation to the institution and mine crossed paths at crucial junctures, even if they did not exactly converge or overlap. I regret to say that I cannot name these junctures with any specificity now.

Come matriculation, Livingstone students' paths would diverge. Of those among my colleagues who were college-bound (and there were very few of us out of the 113 students in the class of 1980 who pursued a tertiary education), most were headed west. For my part, I was on my way to the dual-medium institution.[14]

Like Livingstone, UWC's rugby team was dominated by Afrikaans-speaking students. I am deeply grateful that UWC's curriculum did not regulate for intramurals between the English and Afrikaans majors. I'd had my fair share of bumps, bruises, and deflated athletic ego—enough to last a lifetime. In any case, those UWC Afrikaans[15] majors would have pummeled us.

Leaving Livingstone Behind

And so, after Livingstone, I was heading east. I was going, according to the Livingstone hierarchy, in the wrong institutional direction. I had no qualms, as I was happy just to be going to university—"college," in U.S. parlance.

When I first set foot on the UWC campus, I had no trouble finding my way around. Going from one class to another was easy. Negotiating the campus was effortless because UWC had only five lecture halls. The first four were named, unimaginatively, A, B, C, and D. The fifth was for the sciences, where UWC trained some of the country's finest dentists. UCT, for its part, prepared its charges for the upper echelons of white, liberal South African society.

To its chagrin, UWC's geographical location, on the eastern edge of the windswept plain that is the Cape Flats, gives a certain truth to the pejoration "Bush." The hardy, scrub-like vegetation (wild grasses, Port Jackson trees) gave scant protection when the wind would whip across its dusty flatness. Students quickly learned that on a windy day, it was best to keep one's calves and face covered. On a windy day, the grains of sand kick up sharply. The grains sting. To put it another way, on such a day, one feels as though one is indeed out in the bush.

Early in February 1981, on a bright late-summer day, fresh out of Livingstone and feeling the world full of prospect, I had no such concerns. Into one of my first classes, in Lecture Hall B at UWC, strode a tall, bespectacled man. He was rather energetic and had a smile—one I would later find out to be mischievous—to greet all within his ambit. In his university days, Stan Ridge had been a thespian. (Stan graduated from the University of Natal, another, if less psychically secure, bastion of white liberal privilege.) Stan's acting skills, as I would learn through the years, were consummately honed; he retained these skills throughout the course of his life and could call on them at the drop of a hat, always with impeccable timing. Not only was he, when the moment demanded it, given to theatrical flourish, but he could also adopt any accent—a Scottish brogue, an Irish lilt—as though it were a matter of no consequence.

A Stan Ridge Joke, as Recounted by Elaine Ridge

I knew Stan as a good storyteller. After his passing, I remarked to his wife, Elaine, that I had been entertained by him on many an occasion with a fine tale. However, what I did not know was that he was an expert pilferer of other people's stories.

According to Elaine, Stan was not only adept at nicking other people's stories and passing them off as his own. No, Stan Ridge, a highly valued and model citizen of UWC, a member of good standing in the Stellenbosch community, an upstanding and much

respected figure in the Methodist church he and Elaine attended,
was a shameless appropriator of other people's stories.

As Elaine tells it, he would even proceed to share his pilfered nar-
rative goods—only lightly repurposed—with the very persons from
whom he'd lifted the story.

On one such occasion, as Stan was merrily holding forth, Elaine
tried to warn him, by kicking him lightly on the shin, that he was
now relating a tale with authority to the very person whom he had
relieved of ownership of this story. On charged Stan, happily regal-
ing the assembled company with his "authentic" tale.

He first ignored Elaine; then, when her admonitions became too
insistent to ignore, he turned to her, irritated, and asked: "Would
you like to tell the story?" Caught between the narrative frying pan
and the "thief's" fire, Elaine demurred. There was nothing for her
to do except let Stan finish the story, either oblivious or indifferent
to his wife's attempt to spare him the charge of narrative larceny.

Little of his theatricality was on display on that first day, but his presence in that crowded lecture hall has remained with me, these many
years later. Faced with a cluster of eager English I students, all of us fresh
from high school and in the thrall of the freedom of university life (no
more mandatory school uniforms; jeans every day, if you like; being able
to choose our own subjects, make our own timetables, attend or skip
classes just as we wished), Stan commanded the room.

It is no wonder, then, that my introduction to Stanley Gordon Moysey Ridge was a memorable one. After all, in his presenting himself and
his understanding of the kind of work we were about to do, in committing himself—metonymically, speaking for the English Department in
its entirety—to us as students, he was giving us a glimpse of freedom,
beyond the right to wear whatever attire we chose, beyond our fidelity
to our schedules (this went beyond attending or skipping class). Stan was
inviting us to think about whether or not our tenure at UWC would
open for us onto freedom that which has "already attuned all comport-
ment to being as a whole."[16] It was Being that Stan was encouraging us
to think. It was an attunement to Being that he was trying to instill in

us.[17] The very possibility of our "being as a whole"—being whole in the world, being in the world as a whole, as I argued earlier—is something the apartheid regime was so determined to deny us. At UWC, in our English lectures at least, it was possible to be attuned in such a way that we could let our Being come into being—the being of our Being in its entirety, as being possible to gain access to in all pedagogical encounters at UWC and beyond. It was nothing less than Being that we were being asked to think for, to think toward.

What came through very clearly on that first day and never wavered until his passing in January 2018 was his deep commitment to this higher order of teaching—that mode of teaching that Heidegger would insist we can only find in and through philosophy. In February 1981, he laid out the English Department's vision. Borrowing from the Oxbridge model of instruction, he emphasized the importance of our tutorials, small classes in which faculty worked on our critical skills, teaching us to read everything from "unseen" poems—a randomly selected poem that would have to be critiqued—to newspaper advertising. I had Ruth Will, poetry whiz, for my tutorial. I definitely did not draw the short straw. I would venture that "tuts," as we predictably abbreviated them, with their face-to-face structure (an average of seven students in a small seminar room), were Stan's ideal form of teaching. In the tutorial, you could get down and dirty with the text. You could really immerse yourself in it. He reveled in this, his preferred form of pedagogical engagement.

However, regardless of his preference for the tutorial format, Stan was a teacher (he was especially bravura in teaching Shakespeare). For Stan, the text was, and I mean this in the most assiduous way, but a prop. I remember his instinctive familiarity with the text. I remember most vividly how he was especially given to the performative when *The Tempest* was the text of the day. Shakespeare's play brought out the anticolonialist in Stan. As we were products of CAD's rote learning, Stan caught us out with his question: "When was South Africa discovered?" We were well-trained in the art of memorization, so our hands shot up. This was easy. We'd been taught this stuff since standard 4. The answer, according to our CAD curriculum, was, as you already know, 1652. That's when Jan van Riebeeck, of the Dutch East India Company, arrived at the Cape of Good Hope (always known to earlier travelers as the Cape of Storms) to establish a halfway station between Europe and India, where there were spices to be had.

(Again, the last four digits of my cell phone are 1652; does apartheid history always win?)

Stan smiled that impish, mischievous smile. It said, that smile of his, "Gotcha."

He disabused us of our CAD misperception, to put it mildly. We had been made "barbarians" of, after all.

Columbus did not "discover" America; neither did Amerigo Vespucci. Van Riebeeck certainly did not "discover" a land that had been populated by the indigenous San for thousands of years.

Courtesy of Shakespeare, Stan brought us up short.

You did not need chapter and verse in order to make Stan's point. That may be why he would only occasionally point to the text. Sometimes he would even reach for it and take it in hand. When he did so, he was likely to wave it about as though it were a solemn document, which it was, of course. Maybe twice or thrice, in the many years he taught me, did Stan actually read from the text.

In my Honors year (a one-year postgraduate degree offered in South Africa, which followed a three-year BA, à la the British model; during that year, the student specializes in a single subject, and English was mine), I was the only full-time student in the program. (There were three others who attended part-time by going to only the evening classes; out of the five courses, three of them were held in the morning and in those I was alone with the lecturer.) If the tutorial was Stan's ideal, the intensity of this one-on-one encounter, Oxbridge-style, puts to shame any Levisianian notion of confronting the other. I emerged from my seminar with Stan exhausted, spent, in need of respite. Stan smiled as he saw me on my way out the door; it was as though my intellectual exhaustion reflected well on him. It did, but I only wish he hadn't made his pleasure so obvious.

In the main, however, Stan held forth with a benign confidence, eyes glinting behind his rectangular spectacles. He was a gifted administrator, and at UWC, his gifts blossomed because of his abiding commitment to the institution. Stan served as the chair of UWC's English Department before moving on to key posts in the university administration.

His natural milieu, as is surely obvious by now, was the classroom.

Stan commanded the classroom to the extent that he held us as students in the palm of his hand. His pedagogy, however, was edged with something like the merest hint of reproach at any waywardness. He kept us on our toes, peppering us with questions, fully conversant with the critical trends in just about every field. Drawing on his expertise, he taught *The Tempest*, in 1988, as a Shakespearean meditation on European colonialism. He warmed to Caliban's struggle with language, and he related it, never heavy-handedly, to life in apartheid South Africa.

He drew on Jonathan Dollimore's *Radical Tragedy* and elaborated on it, courtesy of Lawrence Stone's *The Crisis of the Aristocracy*.

I read Dollimore and Stone not, as many of my graduate school colleagues in the United States did, in graduate school, but as an undergraduate at UWC. Some of those with whom I attended graduate school never read Dollimore or Alan Sinfield. (I would later warm to the work of Jonathan Goldberg, who plowed many of the self-same furrows Stan had attended to, under very different conditions.) Some of my graduate colleagues were also entirely unaware of the Princeton historian Stone, that author who had once taught on the very campus we now occupied as graduate students. In their defense, my colleagues had narrower specializations.

Strangely, my introduction to Dollimore, Sinfield, and their ilk was another of the benefits of the canon. The canon, whether you want it to or not, insists on breadth, sometimes superficially so but not always. The upshot of the canon is that sometimes the best choice as a student is having no choice at all. You come to know that which you do not necessarily want to know. The canon instructs, regardless of our desire for what it has to offer. The canon pays no heed to the provinciality of our interests; the canon is indifferent to the specific line of inquiry we wish to pursue within a discipline.

At UWC, I thrilled to the canon as much I chafed against it. I simultaneously immersed myself in it while interrogating its architecture, the moment and mode of its construction, the effects thereof, and, of course, its content. To be instructed in the canon was to know the condition of erasure. For everything you say, you leave several things unsaid. What we were expected to read made us, living as we were under apartheid at UWC, all the more inclined to think that which was excluded. Once more, the dialectic reared its provocative head.

English majors at UWC were thrust into the dialectic because we found ourselves in the midst of faculty who were themselves grappling with similar difficulties, albeit in a higher critical register. There was some comfort in our shared struggle. As students, then, ours was a struggle encouraged—given critical reflection and substance—all the more because of UWC's English Department faculty. When I was a student there, UWC's English Department was composed of the most committed tertiary instructors I have ever encountered.

Our Lecturers

Our teachers were known as lecturers. As university students, we were no longer taught. We were, instead, lectured. (The other reason we designated our teachers "lecturers" may have something to do with the lack of a suitable honorific substitute. In my tenure in UWC's English Department, only one of its members—Stan—had a Ph.D., and as chair of the department, he was also its only professor. We thus could not default, as is the custom in U.S. institutions, to addressing our teachers as "Dr." It was, therefore, "Professor Ridge" and "Mr. Attwell" or "Ms. Barnard." However, some of our lecturers, the aforesaid couple foremost among them, were on their way to completing their dissertations.) The English Department lecturers shaped our intellectual approaches and intensified our apprehensions and uncertainties. In addition, these were teachers who were themselves conflicted about the conditions—apartheid, CAD, a mainly white faculty instructing a student body composed overwhelmingly of coloured students—under which they did their work.

None of these ideological complications, however, compromised the quality of the pedagogical work that UWC's English faculty did. In fact, the sheer weight of the political quandary they lived seemed to spur them to even greater pedagogical heights. They did sterling work. I carry their pedagogical imprint still.

To give Foucault an anti-CAD and, simultaneously, a Heideggerian inflection: "There is no experience"—exceptional pedagogy, in this instance—which does not give one to thinking. In this case, it is the thinking about the pedagogical responsibilities that every classroom, every pedagogical encounter, imposes upon every teacher. If, as Heidegger insists in *Was Heißt Denken?*, the teacher must be more teachable than the student, then such an injunction may have a critical prior point of origin. The teacher can only know what it means to be teachable if the teacher was first, as a student, exposed to a teacher or teachers who embodied such pedagogical rigor and possibility. If Heidegger is correct, and I have no reason to doubt that he is, then I have been fortunate twice over. My teachers at both Livingstone and in UWC's English Department were constantly and intently training themselves to be more student than teacher. Often, I would wager, they were doing so while their Heideggerian exemplarity remained entirely unbeknownst to them. It may very well be, and this is a pedagogical paradox of the first order, that it is the student alone who can determine if the teacher is most teachable. What is more, the erstwhile student may only come to know this after encountering Heidegger's *Was Heißt Denken?* This hardly seems fair. The teacher who was teachable only comes to know of their self-teachability, at least in a formal sense, after—and because of—a former student's recognition.

This is hardly fair. But, Heidegger might intone, no doubt in a stentorian voice, this is why it matters so much that we think about thinking. To be drawn to Heidegger, to be taken with Foucault and Derrida too, it has often seemed to me, has much to do with their deep commitment to teaching. I always apprehend Heidegger and Foucault as masters of the classroom. And this may very well be the reason: In order to teach, it is necessary first to think and second to understand the classroom as that place where thinking must be not only encountered but designated the primary order of pedagogical business. And to think, as I have already said, is the work of the intellectual.

My teachers, regardless of the itinerary of names we called them, were intellectuals. I was taught by intellectuals.

David Attwell taught me African and South African literature. He gave me my first taste of Ngugi wa' Thiongo, Chinua Achebe, Wole Soyinka, Athol Fugard, John Kani, Winston Ntshona, Sembene Ousmane. David gave me his copy of Sembene's *God's Bits of Wood* to read. *God's Bits of Wood* was not available in UWC's library, nor was it available for purchase in any of the bookstores I perused in Cape Town. Once more, the deprivations of studying at a "Bush" college were brought home to me. UWC had one[18] library; UCT had several.

David would later move from UWC to the University of Natal, Pietermaritzbug campus (not the Durban one), before going on to teach at York University in the north of England, where he would later, before retiring (back to Cape Town), become head of York's English Department. There was something appropriate about David finding his way to the city of York, in the county of Yorkshire. After all, Yorkshire is, together with Lancashire (when they play each other, it is dubbed the "War of the Roses"), the very cradle of working-class English cricket. David, after all, was a stylish opening batsman who had played his cricket in Cape Town for Pinelands.

If I had had my first brush with Coetzee at Livingstone, I would find myself much closer to the Nobel Laureate because of David. Dr. David Attwell (who got his Ph.D. from the University of Texas at Austin, the same institution that had decades earlier awarded Coetzee his) was the South African academic most closely associated with J. M. Coetzee.

When Coetzee won the Nobel Prize in 2002, David accompanied him to Stockholm for the ceremony. His erstwhile UWC colleague Rita Barnard (they shared an office) still teases David about having to buy a tuxedo in order to attend the Nobel ceremony. Rita, for her part, received her Ph.D. from the English Department at Duke University, an institution at which I would later teach—not in the English Department, but in Duke's Program in Literature. In a strange and circuitous way, in a delayed fashion, I had followed my UWC lecturer from UWC to Durham, North Carolina.[19]

Ruth Will (now Ruth Roberts) and Micki Flockemann taught me, in my first and second years, respectively, poetry. They were exceptional teachers. Ruth is a fine reader, and she instructed with a controlled, disciplined passion. Micki sharpened my appreciation for Gerard Manley Hopkins. "The Windhover" remains to me unforgettable, full of grammatical precision and invention. What is more, it is minimalist to a fault. With Hopkins, one was instructed into the grammatical magic that words could be made to perform. With Hopkins, one marvels: *Who knew this word, this adverb, this noun, could do that work?*

Rita Barnard told me in the summer of 2022 that she planned to soon retire from teaching American Literature at the University of Pennsylvania, the only academic position she has held since graduating from Duke. She lectured us in Whitman, Emerson, and Thoreau. We read American Literature in English II. (English II should be understood here as second-year English. UWC did not offer electives. Ours was a hierarchical structure so that every course in every subject at UWC took students, step by step, with increasing difficulty, through its own canon— English I–III, History I–III. You were taught the canon as though there was nothing outside of it. In other words, the canon *was* all you needed to know.) Rita taught American literature in such a way that she was always able to intersperse her lectures with popular cultural asides. I remember one lecture, during my first class on a Monday morning in 1982, on Emerson, in which she found a way to connect Thoreau to *E.T.*, the movie. She was somehow able to join her carefully calibrated reflections on Emersonian alienation, individualism, and democracy to an alien who had lost its way in the galaxy. In the milieu that Rita created, it was possible for the lost alien to make contact with earth. In Rita's class, E.T. was given license to "phone home."

In her lectures, Rita held forth with nothing less than élan. Bright, energetic, a former beauty queen, and a working model (she was most known for her TV work for a brand of margarine called Blossom), she made her Monday morning lectures a riveting experience.

David Bunn, who whetted my appetite for the tragic poetry of South African émigré Arthur Nortje, was at that time, like Jane Taylor, working toward his Ph.D. (which both he and Jane would later complete) at Northwestern University in Evanston, Illinois. (Always weighed down by his overstuffed brown leather bag, David gave lectures that were pol-ished, thoughtful, buoyed by a kindness, and amplified by the most gen-tle laugh.)

Jane Taylor dressed with the kind of flair that only a drama specialist could command. If David's laugh was gentle but not quite to the point of being apologetic, Jane's was infectious—grand, sweeping, drawing all into its ambit. That laughter, however, could not entirely disguise her toughness as a teacher. Jane, it seems to me even now, was always mining for one more nugget, always undertaking the search for one more possible meaning that could be extracted from the text. Such was her radiance that as students, we duly did our best to unearth that nugget, to summon up that elusive last, nominally speaking, meaning.

Peter Kohler, who, like Stan, hailed from the University of Natal, dis-guised his smarts as laconic wit. Julia Martin, now a professor (with UWC Ph.D. in hand), guided me toward the pleasures of *Sir Gawain and the Green Knight*. (Julia is the only person still on the faculty from my time there.) The late Patrick Cullinan, a poet of local renown, made me wise to the dissembling that is the poetry of that faux New England farmer, Robert Frost.

I was taught by teachers.

A Final Thank-You to the Teachers Who Taught Me

It is little wonder that I remain, to this day, nothing but a teacher who has before him the model of Morgan MacArthur. I understand that I was privileged to have imbibed something of the spirit of R. O. Dudley. In the intellectual hierarchy that is my apartheid education, Livingstone would rank, among my high school peers, above UWC. Livingstone was, before my time and for a long time afterward, an elite institution, apart-heid or no.

However, this I can assert without fear of being contradicted by my-self: Livingstone laid the foundation upon which my apartheid under-graduate education and my U.S. Ivy League training would be founded. At UWC, however, I felt released into learning, I found joys previously unimaginable, and I found teachers who gave everything.

That I found these things under the condition known historically as apartheid is the consequence of both a perverse dialectic (the commitment of my teachers was disproportionate to the intended "barbarism" of the apartheid regime's educational structure) and a logic that was unimpeachable—education mattered, so material strictures were not so much reduced to nothing as they were approached as obstacles, mere obstacles.

My thinking—all my thinking, every act of thinking I undertake— derives from my apartheid education.

It seems to me now, as it must have in moments of clarity when I was a high school and a university student, that it is only right that I should, given that I have so long been contemplating my apartheid education (I am intrigued but not haunted by it; it is the mold out of which I emerged, but it is a mold that I have tried to break rather than venerate), find the language in which to articulate the perversity of my gratitude.

This kind of gratitude is crafted in and out of thinking. It is the ability to take joy in a thinking given life by the archive in which Heidegger and R. O., Deleuze and Mrs. MacArthur, Kant and Stan keep each other company. This is the kind of thinking that is only able to emerge from perversity. Here, once more, I align entirely with Foucault: It is the experience gifted to me by my teachers that alerted me to the absolute necessity of thinking.

I think, even if, following Heidegger, I do not know what thinking is, because all the important teachers in my life I could not but incline toward thinking.

To have been exposed to this experience, then, imposed a singular responsibility: To learn thinking; to learn to think; to learn, again and again, to think; to produce, out of my experiences, a language, as I have written elsewhere, that can bear thinking, the considerable but always transformative (at least, potentially so) weight of thinking.

To think, perchance to think.

In that formulation, laden with hesitation as it is, informed by the importance of risking what is in order to think, Heidegger lends philosophical inflection to Shakespeare.

That formulation cannot, and I do not intend it to, disguise the many pedagogical spirits out of which it is crafted. In that formulation, my

English teachers Morgan MacArthur and Stan Ridge cohabit with R. O. Dudley.

History, apartheid history, as irony would have it, could not have chosen for me a more veritable, honorable, and inspiring trio of teachers. Each of my teachers, in every encounter with them (if I might be permitted a final hubristic flourish), made of my time with them an event called thinking.

Concepts 5

The Dialectic

It is only at the most superficial level that the dialectic can be understood as the antagonistic encounter between two opposing forces—what we know as the conflict between "thesis" and "antithesis." In truth, however, the dialectic resolves nothing. At the very least, whatever resolution (synthesis) the dialectic yields is, at best, of a temporary nature.[1] Instead, what emerges out the resolution (that is not a resolution) is the production of a new set of contestations that are created from within the resolution itself. The effect of this new set of contestations is to lead us away from the conflict spawned by the original thesis and antithesis. The dialectic is, in this way, both infinitely generative and, in technical terms, infinitely expansive. The new formation that the dialectic assumes leads to the uncovering of new tensions. The dialectic directs our thinking to terrain previously unexplored—unexplored because it was not constitutive of the original thesis and antithesis.

However, achieving distance from the original conflict does not mean that the original conflict disappears. On the contrary, it is subsumed into/by the new dialectical formation, contributing to the rearrangement of forces within this new dialectic; and, in its being subsumed, in its being rearticulated, new conflictual possibilities accrue to it, allowing the original theses and antitheses to reemerge, either in their original or a mutated form.

These dialectical possibilities, infinite and infinitely variable, reveal the core Hegelian concept *Aufhebung*. Generally translated as "sublation," Aufhebung is that understanding of the dialectic that allows for both the thesis and the antithesis to be simultaneously present in the same object. Aufhebung thus makes it possible for the dialectic to simultaneously elevate and lower an object, enabling the object to be at once potentially transcendent and lowered, to rise above and to find itself returned into the original order of things.

This Hegelian fluidity is crucial to *The Perversity of Gratitude* because it contains within it the possibility of constant movement, of tensions always rearranging themselves, and of forces realigning in predictable and unexpected ways. The dialectic here as a set of forces made unpredictable by their encounters, all of which makes it difficult, if not impossible, for these forces to hold onto either their individual identities or their dialectical characteristics—that is, the dialectic is that which emerges out of the ever-present mutation of forces. This ever-present mutation disrupts, does violence to, and disfigures the individual forces in their self-understanding and in the way that they orient themselves in their dialectical relations.

Memory

Memory is the remembering of a past event. More than that, memory is the practice of recollection underwritten by veracity. Memory is the "truth"—the presentation of recollection that insists upon itself as the authoritative representation of the unfolding of events. Memory is the truth of the past. *The Perversity of Gratitude* evokes and mobilizes memory as a counterintuitive force. The memory of a disenfranchised apartheid education is retrieved here not to confirm the violence of a CAD education; that has long since been well-known and circulated widely within anti-apartheid communities. The violence of an IAD education is not in dispute. Memory works here not even to bring to life—to light—the kernel of thinking that was lodged within a CAD education, although it certainly does that too.

Instead, *The Perversity of Gratitude* strips memory of its commonsense so as to reveal the surprising intellectual processes that were put into motion precisely because of the violence that the apartheid regime intended its policies to enact on the disenfranchised mind. The dominant memory of a CAD education is drawn into question and rendered a façade not because of what it revealed but because of what it concealed. In this way, the disenfranchised's memory of their gutter education is shown to be at best superficial (subject to the apartheid regime's dominant narrative) and at worst an exercise devoid of self-reflexivity. Or, differently phrased, to hold with the logic of a gutter education beyond a certain critical point marks an intellectual failure. (What constitutes that critical point is, of course, a matter that would be very difficult to identify. In fact, to mark this critical point, it may indeed be better to rely on intuition—in Heidegger's sense that the point could be known without being named exactly—than on any narrowly scientific measure.) Trusting to anti-apartheid memory, then, constitutes the failure to think.

Memory is the intellectual failure is the failure to think the thinking that could not, arguably, have come into being without apartheid. It is the failure to recognize that, under certain conditions, the disparity in material resources might in fact not be an impediment but a spur to thinking, which is itself a testament to both pedagogy and political commitment. And these are in all likelihood related. A better resourced classroom and a more secure physical plant may very well be able to produce thinking. But there is no a priori guarantee that it will, and the opposite holds within it the same potentialities; a poorly resourced classroom, a decrepit physical plant, so rendered because of a state's (or controlling body's) determination to under-educate a subjugated community, can sometimes present objective but not intellectual difficulties for the work of thinking. It follows, then, that it is equally true that the political commitment to under-resourcing disenfranchised communities, regardless of the pedagogical commitment of teachers, does not guarantee that there will be thinking.

Memory, then, is that understanding of what was that must be confronted but not, under any circumstances, be granted final or absolute authority when the work of thinking is the question that is placed before it. Memory, then, is that which must not, in and of itself, be trusted. Memory is shaded by hues of truth that can, when thinking is in question, dissemble because it has already decided on what was.

Memory is that recollection of things that thinking must, in order to secure its standing, risk doing violence to.

Thinking is opening up memory to more than just the possibility of putting things together, of assembling a series of events, in an entirely new and different way.

It is not simply a matter of re-membering, as certain lines of argument would insist. It is, rather, a matter of taking things apart entirely—of not trusting memory, at least not trusting any memory, no matter its intensity (how viscerally a certain event can be recalled) and affective power (recollecting what it meant to oppose apartheid), that has not been subjected to thinking.

The only memory that should be afforded any standing is that which has been thought.

Apartheid

Thinking apartheid, thinking and apartheid: Two modes of being at once opposed to each other and inextricably bound up in each other. The same is true of every other concept in its relation to apartheid. The effect of these relations, in their multiplicity, in their variegation, in their dialectics, is that apartheid emerges in *The Perversity of Gratitude* in two distinct ways. Apartheid figures first, in its more predictable, bureaucratic guise, as a series of institutions, structures, and processes and as an articulation of raced power. Second, and this is a direct consequence of conceptual interrelatedness, apartheid emerges as an animating force.

If there is no constitutive outside to apartheid, then it must be acknowledged that apartheid manifests itself in every human practice. It is not only a proscription—a series of laws that delineate precisely what the enfranchised and the disenfranchised can do. It is a force that extends its reach beyond the bureaucratic and into every facet of life. Apartheid is, literally, that which gives life to thinking; it brings thinking to light and to life.

Apartheid is, then, in the most complicated sense, an actor in *The Perversity of Gratitude*. As Foucault teaches, power acts not *on* but *through* subjects, so apartheid sets in motion a series of relays. Say, most obviously, oppositional pedagogy ↔ thinking; this is a two-way process because it is not only that an oppositional pedagogy produces thinking but that this process can easily be understood in reverse; oppositional pedagogy could as easily derive from thinking.

As much as anything, *The Perversity of Gratitude* testifies to the lived effects of apartheid as a life force. The act of thinking against apartheid has its roots in the ways in which apartheid makes its presence felt. Apartheid acts, it makes itself a presence—if not always a palpable presence—that is felt by and in the disenfranchised self. Apartheid is embodied in praxis so that apartheid is the other to which the disenfranchised self is opposed. Through its actions, apartheid sets in motion a potential dialectic, compelling the disenfranchised self to respond. Even if the disenfranchised self decides not to respond, it is still responding because it has decided to *do* nothing. In this way, we can say that apartheid inflects—we might even say *infects*—every aspect of disenfranchised life.

Distilled to its essence, *The Perversity of Gratitude* is an act of apartheid. At the very least, this writing is an act of thinking, first and foremost, provoked—or is it produced?—by apartheid.

Responsibility/Irresponsibility

The biblical Abraham is, for Jacques Derrida, a study in irresponsibility. Abraham is a remarkable figure for Derrida because Abraham owes fidelity only to God/g-d. Abraham's obedience to God is such that he dissembles to his wife, Sarah, and is willing to sacrifice their only son (begotten late in life by Sarah), Isaac. Abraham is, in Derrida's rendering, utterly irresponsible, confounding all familial (it is the duty of the parent to protect their offspring) and political (the father does not put his son to death) logic. Indeed, Abraham could be said to openly flout a founding tenet of all monotheisms ("Thou shalt not kill").

In a much lower key, *The Perversity of Gratitude* hews to the Derridean logic of irresponsibility. It will not tarry with conventional notions of anti-apartheid responsibility. *The Perversity of Gratitude* is, in Derrida's sense, irresponsible to hegemonic expectations of CAD education because of its fidelity to thinking. Paradoxically, however, such irresponsibility is indebted entirely to responsibility. Fealty to thinking can only come into being because of those figures (teachers) and institutions (Livingstone, UWC) who were so utterly responsible for teaching thinking.

There can, in this writing, be no irresponsibility that is not firmly grounded in responsibility—if, that is, responsibility is understood as locating the anti-apartheid self (student/teacher) felicitously in relation to itself as a figure dedicated to struggling against the strictures imposed by apartheid bureaucracy, broadly conceived as it is in the previous concept.

Responsibility and irresponsibility, then, are not always in conflict; in fact, there are moments when they function complementarily. One derives from the other. One brings to the fore capacities unintended in the other. Aufhebung of a particular order.

IV

Richard Moore Rive

Tiananmen Square Day

For some of us must storm the castles
Some define the happenings.

—**Arthur Nortje,** "Native's Letter"

June 4th, 1989, that is the day I left South Africa. Once and for all.

Richard Rive, a short story writer, novelist, and essayist, obtained an M.A. from Columbia University, courtesy of Fulbright, and a Ph.D. from Magdalen College in Oxford, where Arthur Nortje, who belonged to the generation of disenfranchised writers who followed Rive, had died, ostensibly by suicide, although the coroner returned an open verdict. Nortje's great gift to Rive was two lines of poetry of which Richard was very fond and often quoted: "For some of us must storm the castles/Some define the happenings." Richard invoked this couplet, I am sure, because it crafted for him, as an anti-apartheid writer, a political role that aligned with his literary predilections. Ballasted by Nortje's injunction to "define the happenings," Richard reveled in his political role, a role that did not demand that the writer undertake the work of physically attacking the ramparts of apartheid.[1] To Rive's mind, Nortje did not so much grant an anti-apartheid writer such as Rive political "absolution" (not every member of the disenfranchised was tasked with or expected to "storm the castles") as he did make a poetic case for the division of political labor. Nortje presented the writer's work as, say, Leninist (the writer as critical to the formation of the vanguard class) or Du Boisian (the writer as a key figure within the ranks of the Talented Tenth). A question that has continued to preoccupy me. Who is assigned by history the task of "storming the castles" and who is designated the work of "defining the happenings?" Does the former, undertaken by the activist, relieve the intellectual of the responsibility to act? Why should acting and thinking be conceived as mutually exclusive?

It seems appropriate to me now that Rive warmed so to his role as "definer of the happenings," because he was the most formally educated disenfranchised person I came to know in apartheid South Africa. I met Richard in January 1988, so I knew him for less than a year and a half. He was murdered in his own home on Tiananmen Square Day. A closeted gay man, he'd gone cruising and picked up two young men who then brutally stabbed him to death. This happened in his own home—a home I had visited several times. It happened in his home, where I had encountered him as a teacher but also as a raconteur, a friend, and a worldly man of letters.

Richard had a study full of books. On our first meeting, he showed me copies of works by famous African authors—Ngugi, Achebe, Soyinka, Amos Tutuola—inscribed to him. They were prized possessions. Works by South African authors too, adorned his shelves, similarly inscribed: Jack Cope, Ingrid Jonker, Nadine Gordimer, James Matthews. He kept up with younger local authors, too—Menan du Plessis, a novelist, and Donald Parenzee, a poet. I spent many hours in his study, where he introduced me—personally, in a sense—to the African authors, just names (famous names, yes) on a dust jacket. He introduced them to me, those African writers I had come to admire. And then there was Richard's deep bond with Langston Hughes, his literary idol, whom he had met. Richard had read Hughes, Countee Cullen, Sterling Brown, Arna Bontemps. Rive, the son of an American sailor, conceived out of wedlock with a coloured woman, evinced a certain pride about being an American, no matter the circumstances of his birth, no matter that he never knew his father. The Harlem Renaissance was Richard's touchstone literary experience. It was through his love for the Harlem Renaissance and Hughes' poetry in particular, one suspects, that Rive was able to not only able to maintain a bond with his father's homeland but also allowed him to mediate his interest in Hughes, an interest that was not purely literary.

Rive told stories about meeting Tutuola, the Nigerian author of *The Palm Wine Drunkard*, and about his first meeting with a (then) young James Ngugi. Richard was a spinner of literary yarns, a man who loved to tell a story. He explained to me why, when the firebrand poet Dennis Brutus inveighed against his fellow South African exile Ezekiel Mphaphlele for returning home to Johannesburg from his appointment at the University of Pennsylvania, Brutus was wrong. "Zeke was homesick, simple as that," Richard told me. (When my UWC teacher Rita Barnard joined the faculty at the University of Pennsylvania, she was assigned Mphaphlele's old office.) Richard held Mphaphlele in high esteem, considering him (and the exiled Peter Abrahams, who then lived in Jamaica) the dean of urban black South African writing. The Protest Writers, as they were known, were an organization of writers that owed much to the publication of Mphaphlele's autobiographical *Down Second Avenue*. The Protest Writers were composed of two groups of disenfranchised authors—one in Johannesburg, one in Cape Town. The Johannesburg group, which included, among others, Mphaphlele, Bloke Modisane, and Nat Nakasa, was composed mainly of what the apartheid state then considered "Native" authors and had strong links to a publication called *Drum Magazine*. (Abrahams, the author of *Tell Freedom* and *Mine Boy*, was the progenitor of this movement. Although he hailed from Johannesburg, he was coloured. The only other coloured author from Johannesburg was Don Mattera.) The coloured writers Rive, Matthews, and the Marxist Alex la Guma made up the Cape Town wing of the movement.

Richard and I used to meet, on average, once every other week. Through our exchanges, I was educated in an entirely new literary canon that was distinct from my Livingstone English syllabus as well as what was on offer at UWC. I did indeed read, as I have said, some African literature—mainly anti- and postcolonial literature by African authors who hailed from south of the Sahara. In my Honors English course, I read—with David Bunn, as I said—Nortje, whom Richard had known and, in typical Richard fashion, claimed to have mentored, at least a little, at any rate. This was an endearing Richard trait: Staking a claim to mentorship or influence. The white South African writer Menan du Plessis, who came to prominence in the mid- to late 1980s, considered him, rather than future Nobel laureate J. M. Coetzee, to be her primary influence, Richard remarked to me more than once. A simple glance at du Plessis's work would suggest otherwise.

It was one thing to have read or to have written on Nortje, the South African playwright Athol Fugard, or the exiled poet Jennifer Davids; it was another to have them rendered by Richard.

Livingstone and UWC had opened worlds for me that I came to know and love. I was glad to have been educated in the canon—Keats, Yeats, Woolf, *Sir Gawain and the Green Knight*, Chaucer, Whitman, Ralph Ellison, Poe, Emerson, George Eliot, Eliot, Ford Maddox Ford, Faulkner; I even learned, despite Patrick Cullinan's best efforts, to tolerate Robert Frost and I remain smitten with John Milton. How I found myself totally consumed in *Paradise Lost*. After my final English III exam, in which there had been a choice between American literature and Milton, I ran into Stan on campus. "What did you write on?," he asked. "Milton," I replied, unable to keep the thrill out of my voice. In true Stan fashion, he was quick to make mischief. "You are of the Devil's party, Grant, and you know it."

However misguided, I had a strong sense of "knowing" the canon. Apartheid education will do that to you, whether it intends to or not. Richard, too, opened a world to me. But there was a difference. He was a living, breathing, disenfranchised writer. He was published and widely regarded. Richard taught English at a local teacher's training college, Hewat. He knew Shakespeare and loved to quote him; "This castle hath a noble seat," he was quick to quip. He had been to and studied in New York and had traveled widely because of his work—not only in Africa and Europe, but in Japan too. At his core, I am now inclined to believe, he was a man of the canon. Richard acquired a faux Oxbridge accent, much commented upon by those in his circle and sometimes the butt of jokes. But his political commitment, his experience as a disenfranchised author, demanded otherwise. And so he threw himself into it.

R. O. was an intellectual of the first order. Stan, a teacher from his hair-parting to his toenails, possessed a keen, ironic intellect.

But Richard was different.

This was a world from which disenfranchised South Africans, in the main, were shut out. It was a world where Ngugi, Soyinka, and Achebe (another Rive favorite) held court. That is the world that Richard opened up for me and made *real* for me. He would invite me to accompany him to soirees where I, still a UWC graduate student, watched from a safe distance as Richard hobnobbed his way around the room, clearly a central figure in the who's who of Cape Town's literary high society. It was heady stuff, I know now. Back then, I was simply unbelieving, watching novelists, poets, editors, and academics from UWC and UCT and bigwigs from the then-burgeoning NGO world interact. *This is what it meant to be an intellectual—a black intellectual, a disenfranchised black intellectual living the condition, the difficulty, the intense contradiction, that was the diaspora-in-place.*

I heard stories about Achebe's gentle demeanor and stories about Tutuola, in all likelihood apocryphal, appearing at a conference in the United States with bells on his toes. I heard of Richard's difficult relationship with Brutus, whom he considered, at the very least, mean-spirited and dogmatic. In my single public encounter with Brutus, in August 1992, I got a glimpse of why Richard kept his distance from Brutus. A sure-footed poet, Brutus was doctrinaire in his outlook, devoid of nuance and subtlety in his politics. He was anachronistic too, clinging angrily to a set of principles made redundant by the rapidly changing world that was preparing itself to be postapartheid, putatively democratic South Africa. In truth, Brutus was not wrong in his fears. Brutus sensed that in the ANC's dispensing with the principles that had sustained the anti-apartheid activists such as Brutus for so long, a postapartheid society made unequal no longer by race but by access to capital would emerge. Dennis Brutus was not wrong. He knew that the face of the new South Africa would be, in the old apartheid parlance, "multiracial." The fruits of the struggle, as is so often the case with postcolonial societies, would be reaped by those who best knew how to position themselves in relation to power—Williams's "new men" come to postapartheid life.

Brutus was simply incapable of mounting a second line of attack, and for that he cannot be blamed. This time, Brutus knew, he would have to do battle against those who until just yesterday he numbered among his comrades. Realpolitik, Brutus must have intuited, was about to lay waste to the principled idealism of his anti-apartheid politics. The end of apartheid was not a triumph for Dennis Brutus.[2] It was, for him and for many of his political persuasion (and here I stand firmly with Brutus), a tragedy, and, Iago-like, it was an aspect Brutus bore, if not with relish, then with a dismissive bravura. But it was precisely this sui generis bravura that made one loathe to lament, "Alas, poor Dennis, alas." Brutus did not inspire, in me, at any rate, a Shakespearean empathy of the kind I felt at Richard's brutal death.

In any case, Brutus would surely have considered Richard, with his faux-Oxford accent, pompous. I came to Brutus inflected by Richard's wariness. I was glad of Richard's caution.

Under much more amiable conditions, I would, many years later, meet Ngugi when he visited Duke University to deliver a lecture. Ngugi was seated on a bench by himself, and I approached him with a photo of him and Richard, published in Richard's autobiography, *Writing Black*. Ngugi was touched by the photo, which he'd never seen; a gentle soul, Ngugi was.

My copy of *Writing Black*, and most of his other works, is inscribed by Richard. Those books have traveled with me from Cape Town to New York to the many places I have lived in the United States. I peruse his works from time to time, and when I do, I am almost always moved to smile, recalling one Richard story or another. He is with me still.

The Biography Is Not the Chronicling of a Life; It Is an Account of the Effect of a Life

Richard would have been disappointed that I pursued my graduate work in the United States after Columbia. He would have preferred me to follow his trajectory and head to Oxford, but Oxbridge was the dream, the gold standard, for his generation, not mine.

"The plantations," is how he referred to the United States, much as he loved Hughes, Cullen, and James Weldon Johnson. "*God's Trombones*," Richard would intone, with reverence.

Richard had other plans for me. He wanted me to write his biography. He gave me access to his papers, he showed me where things were. "I keep diaries," he said of his travels, "like other people take photographs."

I, alas, am no biographer. I have written about Richard more than once, but his biography is beyond me.

But I do bear testament to the Rive effect.

Richard could, as I said, be pompous. "Can you spell bourgeoisie?" he was known to inquire of holier-than-thou activists who took issue with the soiree life. But for all that, he was, to my mind at least, although others may disagree, neither patronizing nor condescending. "Sometimes," he would say to me, "you have to stick your B.A. in your back pocket." There remained about him too much of the working-class boy, the fatherless son who'd grown up in District Six, that famed Cape Town community destroyed by apartheid. He refused to bow to the romance that had, in the wake of its destruction and the aftermath of his own deracination, accrued to District Six and made of District Six part idyllic myth (a community composed of many races, all of whom lived harmoniously together), part political rallying cry against the violence of apartheid law. Richard was impatient with this rendering of his birthplace. Instead, he insisted, it was "dirty, dark and dank." Richard was too keenly aware of the path that had led him from District Six to UCT to Columbia and Magdalen (pronounced, Richard was sure to remind everyone, "Maudlin"; in his bathroom there were plaques of all the Oxford colleges).

He knew the perils of working-class life. He had family, including a sister who lived in the same working-class community I did. This sister had a son who Richard helped get a scholarship to Amherst College in the Berkshires, fierce rivals of Williams College, where I later taught.

I would have made, and would still make, a poor Richard Rive biographer. A mutual friend of ours, Shaun Viljoen, who was also Richard's colleague at Hewat Teachers Training College, has done an admirable job.

But Richard's effect on me is indisputable. He was the first disenfranchised intellectual I met. I had never met anyone like Richard before our first encounter. Richard mapped for me, with great deliberateness, a path out of South Africa. He lived for me an intellectual life; he valued books, art, a quiet place to do one's work—Richard lived for me joy that was to be found in that life, and possibly in that life only. Most important, he showed me that it was possible for someone like me to write. That is the enduring effect of not writing his biography.

I recognize the absolute need to write as a mode of being in the world. And to write is, for me, to think. No wonder Richard's favorite Arthur Nortje lines were, as already explicated:

> For some of us must storm the castles
> Some define the happenings.

Whether or not Richard knew it, what I have learned is how difficult it is to "define the happenings." They are elusive, stubborn, resistant creatures, these happenings. Nortje, like Richard an Oxford man (Jesus College), produced and proffered his critiques of the happenings from afar—from England, where he died, from Canada, where pursued a lost love. Nortje was, if anything, a poet as much in struggle with himself as Richard, the closeted gay man, was. Nortje's struggle, as his poetry attests, turned on what he lived as the pathology of being a coloured South African. It seeps everywhere out of his poetry. Nortje was in exile long before he left. I suspect that Nortje, who attended UWC when it was known as the University College of the Western Cape, knew what it meant to live the diaspora-in-place. He also knew what it meant to live an exile of the "Hotel California" variety. Nortje left South Africa, but he never escaped. Perhaps no one does—certainly not alive. That is a tragedy of a far higher order than envisaged in "Hotel California."

No wonder, then, that on Tiananmen Square Day, the die was cast for me. I did not know it then, but I must surely have known it. I must, at least, have, as Heidegger would put it, "intuited" it. I would never return. I would carry Livingstone and UWC's English Department with me. I would always remember the school song. I have, as it were, lived that school song.

But when Richard was murdered—murdered because he was gay— and when his killers got, with as homophobic a defense as one could imagine, the lightest possible sentence (seven years in jail, with the possibility of probation), I knew I would not return.

Richard had planned to retire to a quiet house in Oxford, he used to tell me.

He too must have known that it was important to leave—later rather than sooner, for him; the reverse for me.

He could not have known how much he helped me to leave, how much he made it possible to leave and to live, in Arendt's grand but by no means insincere terms, the "life of the mind."

Whatever debt it is I owe apartheid, and I acknowledge it to be substantial—perverse, yes, but still substantial—I owe my teachers a great deal more.

That South Africa could have laid Richard's life to waste so brutally and be so cavalier in the injustice it dispensed—that was when I knew, irrevocably, I would never return. Migration, I've written elsewhere, is a one-way trip.

It may be that as much intellectual sustenance as the concept and experience that is the diaspora-in-place provides, it is not enough by itself.

With Richard's death, I may have, unbeknownst to myself, considered my debt to the apartheid paid. And if it wasn't, so be it. The ledger would have to remain open.

Tiananmen Square Day was a bloody event, marked by unrestrained Chinese state violence. On the other side of the world, a closeted gay man was viciously stabbed to death. This was a bloody event of a different magnitude. One event is remembered, its effects universal; the other less so—much less so. The death of the gay man is entrusted to the memory of his friends, his students, his old political comrades who survived him. For me, Richard's murder and Tiananmen Square Day will always belong to the same moment—the universal and the particular, joined by the accident of a repressive and brutal history.

The only way to properly recognize this strange historical coincidence, to think its effects, was to leave and then to return to the particular via the written word. The written word is a means of making sense of the perversity of gratitude, of thinking the perversity of gratitude and all the concepts and experience that attend to it.

The Perversity of Gratitude is undoubtedly written in a register I can barely decipher and can surely not name; it is a work that I conceived, at least in part, as a writing to and for Richard—autopoiesis of a variety inflected by Richard Rive. It is a writing that may have begun, unaware of it though I was, in Richard's study. *The Perversity of Gratitude* is, as such, derived from and written in a spirit that is not alien to the one that animates his *Writing Black*.

R. O. lived literally less than a mile from Richard in Windsor Park (which borders directly Elfindale, where R. O. lived), an upper-middle-class coloured neighborhood in Cape Town's southern suburbs. The two Richards, Richard Owen and Richard Moore, knew each other, if not at a distance, then certainly at a polite remove. Nonetheless, they were, each in their own way, agents of Unity Movement thinking. R. O. was its leader, and Richard was a garrulous occasional fellow traveler. Their intellectual circles overlapped only now and then, but they belonged, finally, to different worlds.

In material terms, R. O. and Richard shared a class status. R. O., however, bore his standing with ease, as befits the son of a highly regarded teacher, the son who would go on to outstrip the father in accomplishment and recognition, the son who would himself become the father of a medical doctor (R. O.'s daughter, Nerene) and two professional sons (Gary, a teacher, and Russell, an NGO activist). For all Richard's pride in being a "Magdalen Man," there was always about him a certain vulnerability, a certain lack of ease—perhaps the kind of social unease that clings, despite every effort to shuck it off, to the abandoned son. A gay man who never came out, Richard was outed only in and because of his death,[3] which leads to the closeted gay man comporting himself with braggadocio—the adopted accent, the capacity to marshal the English language with panache and a marvelous, endearing theatricality, his ability to command a room—that could not but perform its own tragic aspect. Alas, poor Richard. Alas.

It was Stan who insisted that I contact Richard once I decided to pursue graduate work in the United States. It was Stan, in a very subdued voice, who confirmed Richard's death for me on that bloody Sunday.

It is in Richard, then, that my teachers converge.

R. O., Mrs. MacArthur, and Stan instructed me on the intellectual value of perversity, a value that I may now inscribe with its own perverse virtue—not an unimpugnable virtue but a flawed virtue, maybe, if such a creature might be imagined?

I cannot decide if Richard urged me explicitly or simply asked me wordlessly to trust myself to writing. Since he lined me up as his biographer, it must have been explicit, but I must have known then already that if I was to write, it would be a different kind of writing I would have to pursue.

But of this, of this, I am sure: Richard Rive, who had written books, showed me why writing mattered. Only writing can bear thinking. Only by thinking perversely, only out of thinking perversity, is it possible to give voice to gratitude for apartheid.

Notes

PREFACE

1. Jacques Derrida, *Monolingualism of the Other Or The Prosthesis of Origin*, trans. Patrick Mensah (Stanford, CA: Stanford University Press, 1998), 1. This struggle with how to live with a language that is not his will later in the text find an equally rich formulation. Derrida names this condition an "inalienable alienation" (Derrida, *Monolingualism*, 25).

2. I have written about Jacques Derrida as a figure of and for African thought in an earlier work: *The Burden of Over-representation: Race, Sport and Philosophy* (Philadelphia: Temple University Press, 2018). I address many of the issues about Derrida's relationship to the French language that he raises in *Monolingualism* in *The Burden of Over-representation*; however, as the invocation of that difficulty again here would suggest—made especially evident by the placement of a quote from that text as the framing device for *The Perversity of Gratitude*—it is a problematic that continues to preoccupy my thinking.

3. The National Party (NP), the architects of apartheid, came to power in 1948 but it would take at least until the mid-1950s before the NP consolidated their power. They would, effectively, remain in power until February 1990, although it is only with the first democratic elections in April 1994, that they *de jure* were removed from power.

4. As much as I know that I must have been living for a very long time with the question about what it meant to have been educated as a disenfranchised South African under apartheid—perhaps since I first entered school and arguably even before that—I should acknowledge that the first formal articulation of *The Per-*

versity of Gratitude is to be found in "The Benefits of an Apartheid Education" in my pamphlet, *Martin Heidegger Saved My Life* (Minneapolis: University of Minnesota Press, 2015).

5. I have in mind here Phillipe Lacoue-Labarthe and Jean-Luc Nancy's *The Literary Absolute: The Theory of Literature in German Romanticism*, trans. Philip Barnard and Cheryl Lester (Albany, NY: SUNY Press, 1988), a work in which the fragment operates both as an individuated thought and serially—in its relation to other individuations.

6. The work of philosophy, argue Gilles Deleuze and Félix Guattari, is to create concepts. See Deleuze and Guattari, *What Is Philosophy?*, trans. Hugh Tomlinson and Graham Burchell (New York: Columbia University Press, 1994). As such, *perversity* and *gratitude* are the concepts created in this writing. Deleuze and Guattari, however, presuppose that new conditions call for the creation of new concepts; as such, any concept is, in and of itself, subject to exhaustion. This may very well be the case. However, I would propose that we should mine any one concept as fully as possible before turning to the work of creation, as important as that might be. To that end, *The Perversity of Gratitude* presents its three fundamental concepts in their fecundity, a richness that derives as much from their interplay as it does from how it is they are in relation to other, adjacent concepts—concepts that are not fundamental but are in close proximity to thinking, perversity, and gratitude.

7. See Deleuze, *Difference & Repetition*, trans. Paul Patton (New York: Columbia University Press, 1994).

8. Martin Heidegger makes this assertion in *Was Heißt Denken?* I note this only schematically here because *Was Heißt Denken?* is one of the texts, if not the core text, that provoked *The Perversity of Gratitude* into being and will be engaged more fully, and repeatedly, shortly. Martin Heidegger provides a critique of the unthought in his work *What Is Called Thinking?*, trans. Fred D. Wieck and J. Glenn Gray (New York: Harper & Row, 1968). I take up this issue elsewhere, including most recently in the following issue: Grant Farred and Nicolette Bragg, "The Language that Can Bear Thinking: An Interview with Grant Farred," *Diacritics* 50, no. 2 (June 2023): 52–63.

GRATITUDE

1. White education, needless to say, required no racially specific designation and, as such, fell under the umbrella of the Education Department.

2. To think rupturously is to, as Timothy Campbell and I argue in *The Comic Self: Toward Dispossession* (Minneapolis: University of Minnesota Press, 2023), break things open, to do a violence to convention. It is also, we insist, to invariably raise the possibility of thinking rapturously—that is, to think with a certain joy, an unarguable joie de vivre. Something of that rupturous/rapturous spirit courses through the veins of *The Perversity of Gratitude*.

3. Also sometimes referred as the "history of the present." See Michel Foucault, *The Order of Things: An Archeology of the Human Sciences* (New York: Vintage Books, 1973).

4. Heidegger, *Was Heißt Denken?*, 4.

5. See Frantz Fanon's critique of the national bourgeoisie in the chapter "The Trials and Tribulations of National Consciousness," in *The Wretched of the Earth*, trans. Richard Philcox (New York: Grove Press, 2004).

6. I am indebted for this term to my friend Dirk Uffelmann.

7. Heidegger, *Was Heißt Denken,* Part I.

8. William Shakespeare, *Hamlet* (Oxford: At the Clarendon Press, 1965), 1.5.

9. There are, of course, more pejorative terms that could be invoked, such as *complicity, fifth columnist,* or *collaborator.* But all of these terms would miss the mark because they traffic strictly in denunciation. The philosophical possibilities, complications, and nuances are entirely lost to these terms, precisely because they begin from the ground of condemnation.

CONCEPTS 1

1. Heidegger, *What is Called Thinking?*, 4.

2. For Martin Heidegger, intuition has one key aspect. From his attribution of "*intuius originarius*" ("original intuition") to God, Heidegger concludes that only God is capable of "original intuition" and, as such, "God does not need to think"—"Thinking as such is the mark of finitude." See Michael Inwood, *A Heidegger Dictionary* (Malden, MA: Blackwell Publishing, 1999), 69. Human beings' thinking is a sign of our "finitude."

3. Intuition, as a form of knowledge, is also important to Baruch Spinoza. In *Ethics*, Spinoza proposes three kinds of knowledge: imagination, reason, and intuition. For Spinoza, any one of these forms of knowledge by itself would be inadequate. In order to know, it is necessary to use all these forms. See Spinoza, *Ethics*, in *Spinoza: Complete Works*, trans. Samuel Shirley (Indianapolis, IN: Hackett Publishing Company, 2002).

4. *Dasein*, a term which so dominates Heidegger's work, remains, for all that, incredibly difficult, if not possible, to hold to a single definition. To that end, *Dasein* is proposed as it is the text: encompassing within itself a range of meanings, but all of which return us to what it means to be in the world. See Michael Inwood's *A Heidegger Dictionary* (Malden, MA: Blackwell Publishing, 1999), for a brief overview of the various meanings that can be attached to or extracted from the term.

5. Published in 2014, *Schwartze Hefte* is a collection of some thirty-four notebooks—one is reportedly missing, containing Heidegger's private ruminations—notebooks he is said to have kept by his bedside to jot down thoughts in before he retired. Some of the most revealing passages in the notebooks are those in which he addresses Hannah Arendt, his Jewish former student and lover, about the accusations of antisemitism leveled against him and how it pertains to their relationship.

6. Jacques Derrida, "Heidegger, the Philosopher's Hell," in *Points . . . Interviews, 1974–1994*, trans. Peggy Kamuf and others (Stanford, CA: Stanford University Press, 1995), 183.

7. See Grant Farred, *Martin Heidegger Saved My Life*.

8. Perversity, it is worth noting, is not far from Derrida's thinking in "Heidegger, the Philosopher's Hell": "This is a complex and unstable knot which I try to untangle by recognizing the threads common to Nazism and anti-Nazism, the law of resemblance, the inevitability of perversion." Derrida, "Heidegger, the Philosopher's Hell," 185. If one thinks Heidegger, especially if one tarries with National Socialism for any length of time, it would seem that the only terminus at which one could arrive is "perversion."

9. Derrida, "Heidegger, the Philosopher's Hell," 184.

10. Augustine, *Confessions*, trans. F. J. Sheed (Indianapolis: Hackett Publishing, 2006), 11.

11. Derrida, *La carte postale (The Postcard)*, trans. Alan Bass (Chicago: University of Chicago Press, 2020), 15.

12. Jacques Derrida, *Cinders* (Minneapolis: University of Minnesota Press, 2014).

13. Karl Marx, "The Eighteenth Brumaire of Louis Bonaparte," in *The Karl Marx Library*, vol. 1, ed. Saul K. Padover (New York: McGraw Hill, 1972), 245.

14. Marx, "The Eighteenth Brumaire," 245.

15. Giorgio Agamben, *The Time That Remains: A Commentary on the Letter to the Romans*, trans. Patricia Dailey (Stanford, CA: Stanford University Press), 2005.

16. Alain Badiou, *Saint Paul: The Foundation of Universalism*, trans. Ray Brassier (Stanford, CA: Stanford University Press), 2003.

17. Slavoj Žižek, *The Puppet and the Dwarf: The Perverse Core of Christianity* (Cambridge, MA: Massachusetts Institute of Technology Press), 2003.

18. Jacob Taubes, *The Political Theology of Paul*, trans. Dana Hollander (Stanford, CA: Stanford University Press, 1993). Presented as a series of lectures in 1987, Taubes's work has a certain conversational bravado woven into his often erudite presentation generalizations and declamations, as well as a breeziness. Of Hitler, Carl Schmitt, and Heidegger, Taubes proclaims: "All three are Catholics gone stale" (Taubes, *The Political Theology of Paul*, 103).

19. "The foundation of universalism" is the subtitle of Alain Badiou's *Saint Paul*, trans. Ray Brassier (Stanford, CA: Stanford University Press, 2003).

20. See Martin Heidegger, *Being and Time (Sein und Zeit)*, trans. Joan Stambaugh (Albany, NY: State University of New York Press, 1996). See especially sections 31 and 35, "Da-sein as Understanding" and "Idle Talk." In section 35, Heidegger makes clear that he does not speak of idle talk "in a disparaging sense. Terminologically, it means a positive phenomenon that constitutes the mode of being of the understanding and interpretation of everyday Da-Sein" (Heidegger, *Being and Time*, 157).

21. Martin Heidegger, "On the Essence of Truth," in *Basic Writings: Martin Heidegger*, ed. David Farrell Krell (Toronto: Harper Perrenial, 2008), 130.

CHAPTER I

1. Marx, "The Eighteenth Brumaire," 595.

2. The concept of head boy can be traced to the British public school, institutions such as Eton, Harrow, and Rugby, where the British ruling, generation after generation, was educated. (And continues to be, with the proviso that it now accommodates sons of the ruling elite from both Britain and far beyond.) The head boy is a student in his final year of high school who is appointed to his post by the school's teachers. The head boy is the exemplary senior student who sets the academic and ethical tone for the rest of his class and the school. By the time I arrived at Livingstone, the school appointed both a head boy and a head girl, supported in their duties by a collection of other senior students known as prefects; another vestige of the British public school.

3. For a brief synopsis of Mr. Dudley's biography, which includes a reflection on his role in the anti-CAD movement, see "Richard Owen Dudley," South African History Online, accessed August 29, 2021, https://www.sahistory.org.za/people /richard-owen-dudley.

4. To my mind, South Africa has produced two intellectuals: R. O. Dudley, and the Nobel Laureate for Literature, J. M. Coetzee. That is enough, remarkable as these thinkers are.

5. The South African school system is today divided into two tiers: primary (grades 1 through 7) and high school (grades 8 through 12). When I was a student, however, primary school began with substandards ("sub") A and B, followed by standards 1 through 5; high school began in standard 6 and ended with matriculation—"graduation"—in standard 10. Today, the system, while not having the middle school component many U.S. schools do, has adopted the U.S. nomenclature of "grades" 1–12. Furthermore, whereas we were "students" (or "pupils"), today's South Africa boasts of "learners." "Students" and "pupils," one is left to conclude, were incapable of "learning" and in order to do so had to be renamed.

6. Raymond Williams, "Culture Is Ordinary," in *Resources of Hope: Culture, Democracy, Socialism*, ed. Robin Gable (London: Verso, 1989), 3–4.

7. Williams, "Culture Is Ordinary," 3–4.

8. Williams, "Culture Is Ordinary," 3–4.

9. Williams, "Culture Is Ordinary," 3–4.

10. Williams, "Culture Is Ordinary," 3–4.

11. Williams, "Culture Is Ordinary," 3–4.

12. Antonio Gramsci's full articulation runs: "All men [*sic*] are intellectuals, one could therefore say: but not men have in society the function of intellectuals." Gramsci, *Selections from the Prison Notebooks*, trans. Quentin Hoare and Geoffrey Nowell Smith (New York: International Publishers, 1989), 9.

13. Fredric Jameson, *Sartre: The Origins of a Style* (New York: Columbia University Press, 1984), 9.

14. C.L.R. James, *The Black Jacobins and the San Domingo Revolution* (New York: Vintage Books, 1989).

15. C.L.R. James, *Beyond a Boundary* (Durham, NC: Duke University Press, 1993), 39.

16. It is their pretentiousness—as well as their lack of creativity, their aptitude for imitation without a difference—that makes postcolonial critics such as Frantz Fanon and Walter Rodney so intolerant of this class.

17. Therefore, "nonracism." In a moment in U.S. history, let us name it the *longue durée* that is the United States after George Floyd (May 2020; much as the U.S. state continues its assault on minority life), when the battle cry against the myriad state violences is "antiracist," "nonracist"—or "nonracialism," or "nonracist"—and strikes the U.S. ear as, at best, unfamiliar. Perhaps it even seems anachronistic, as if it belongs to a bygone era (if, that is, the concept of nonracism ever had currency in this society). And that would be accurate. *Nonracism* is a term birthed by the NEUM in the 1940s, but its actual origin is more like 1789—the French Revolution, the Enlightenment. "All men [*sic*] are created equal." Antiracism gathers its rhetorical force from its *oppositionality*; it is opposed to racism. As such, whether it is conceded or not is hardly relevant, as all antiracism a priori gives credence to race. Racism, so conceived, is the (inevitable) practice that derives from the difference among the races.

Let us take W.E.B. Du Bois, for example. For all Du Bois's acumen, he cedes—concedes—race as epistemological and ontological ground. Du Bois begins with the Negro as a *problem*: "The problem of the Twentieth-Century is the problem of the color-line" (Du Bois, 34). The "problem" is assumed to be on unassailable conceptual ground.

This is not so in the terms offered by NEUM. For Du Bois, the problem resides in the unjust way the Negro is treated—subject to violence, disenfranchised, under-educated, condemned to menial labor, and so on. The problem, in the Unity Movement's thinking, is where Du Bois's notion of the problem and the contemporary antiracist struggle in the United States begins. It accepts the category of *race*. That is the problem with Du Bois's problem. Dialectically, if on no other grounds, all talk of a problem as well as all efforts to mount antiracism as an ideological offensive against racism already accede to the existence of race. There can be no antiracism without racism, ergo, there can be no antiracism without race as an extant and, what is more, an *accepted*—explicitly—category of human life.

Unyielding in their fealty to the Enlightenment principle that all men [*sic*] *are* men, are equal in and because of their shared humanity, the Unity Movement makes no accommodation for *race as such*.

The Unity Movement position is the radical kernel of the Enlightenment distilled to the essence of its truth: Human biology is singular, and, as such, there is no category of being except the *human*. For the Unity Movement, race is a colonialist construct devised to subjugate those who do not trace their origins to Europe (adding a certain unexpected élan and intransigence to the *Non-European* in the "Non-European Unity Movement"). Race must, for this reason, be rejected. All political work must be directed at discrediting any and all theories of race—as much, that is, as nonracialism must dedicate itself to undoing the effects of the imposition of the category of race and deleterious consequence that is "racial difference" that flows, inevitably, from ceding the existence of "race" in the first place.

The difference, then, lies in the struggle for the eradication of a practice (antiracism) as opposed to a foundational negation (there is no such thing as race).

We could, of course, argue that anti- and nonracism struggle toward the same broad end: Overcoming and eliminating racism. However, what must not be overlooked is their philosophical point of departure. Refutation is entirely distinct from opposition. For the Unity Movement, any other position would have been untenable because any other form of opposition, such as the ANC's Freedom Charter, which gives credence to apartheid's racial categories, would, implicitly or explicitly, one way or another, have acceded to the "reality" of race as a category—biopolitically, we might say.

18. Heidegger, *Was Heißt Denken?*, 4.

19. Heidegger, *Was Heißt Denken?*, 4.

20. In truth, "Education Before Liberation" constituted, in several ways, an impossible political project. How would one know, to begin with, when the disenfranchised were so universally well-educated that they were now ready to secure their liberation? I exaggerate, of course, but the lack of a vision to simultaneously educate oneself as an oppressed subject and liberate oneself from that oppression proved to be among the key factors in the Unity Movement's undoing; it is the reason why many of those more inclined toward activism abandon the organization in favor of the populist ANC. Combined, these ideological and political factors, inter alia, explain in part the organization's fall into political irrelevance. However, the value of the organization's rigorous intellectual training served many a disenfranchised generation very well. It distinguished even those who later took the populist, nationalist route from their ANC peers.

21. Stuart Hall and Paddy Whannel wrote *The Popular Arts* (London: Hutchinson, 1964) when they were secondary school teachers in England.

22. Leon Trotsky, *Permanent Revolution* (Calcutta: Gupta, Rahman and Gupta, 1947). I regret only that we were not encouraged—or made aware of, for that matter—Trotsky's later work, *The Revolution Betrayed* (Mineola, NY: Dover Publications, 2004). In this later work, Trotsky maintains, despite everything, an abiding faith in the possibility of revolution, but this in no way prevents him from producing a scathing critique of the failed Soviet Revolution sparing no one, especially not Stalin but also not the machinations of an emerging "state capitalism."

23. Jameson, *Sartre*, 102.

24. Jameson, *Sartre*, 102.

25. Georg W. F. Hegel, *The Philosophy of History*, trans. J. Sibree (Amherst, NY: Prometheus Books, 1991), 30.

26. In the Western Cape, there were other coloured high schools where an ethos similar to the one at Livingstone obtained. Such a list would include, but is by no means restricted to, South Peninsula ("SP," in common parlance), Harold Cressy ("Cressy"), Trafalgar High ("Traffs"), Belgravia High ("Bellies"), Athlone High, and Alexander Sinton ("Sinton"). All these schools had teachers who were directly or indirectly affiliated with the Unity Movement (originally known as the Non-European Unity Movement, taking its cue from apartheid's racial designations—see note 3) and the Teachers League of South Africa (TLSA). All of these high schools, which were mainly attended by middle-class coloureds, evinced a radical political culture, the outgrowth of an intellectual ferment geared toward opposing the apartheid regime. All these high schools are located in what used to be exclusively middle-class coloured neighborhoods. Here, Livingstone, South Peninsula, Trafalgar, and Harold Cressy are the exceptions. Livingstone is located at the eastern edge of Claremont (some would also name the neighborhood Harfield or Harfield Village), a suburb that was previously inhabited by South Africans of every racial category, although it housed mainly coloureds until the late 1960s, when the process of deracination began and the area began to trend white due to gentrification. Harold Cressy, for its part, is situated on the lower slopes of Table Mountain (Bo-Kaap), as is Trafalgar (in the area adjoining Cressy, and both schools drew their student body from the famous District Six neighborhood, an area brutally razed by the apartheid regime). "SP" (where Richard Rive taught) is in Plumstead, a neighborhood not dissimilar in character from Harfield. Although all three schools, like Livingstone, were in areas designated for whites only, their history was such that not even the Nationalist Party government, the architects of apartheid, dared to relocate the schools. This does not mean that they did not try, but their efforts came to naught. An alumnus of Trafalgar, Harold Cressy went on to become the first coloured in South Africa to obtain a B.A. degree. He graduated from UCT, and although he died tragically young (twenty-seven), he lived long enough to become one of the founders of the TLSA. As the crow flies, Cressy is not that far from UCT, but it was, for the graduate Harold Cressy, a world far removed.

27. Under apartheid, coloureds were mixed-race South Africans who constituted their own racial category, alongside whites, blacks, and "Indians," South Africans of South Asian descent. In earlier apartheid nomenclature, whites were designated "European" and blacks "Natives" and, after that, "Bantu."

28. Confounding expectation, Dylan gave—in absentia, of course—a rather graceful Nobel acceptance speech, available at https://www.nobelprize.org/prizes/literature/2016/dylan/speech/.

29. "Gotta Serve Somebody," Bob Dylan, accessed July 18, 2023, https://www.bobdylan.com/songs/gotta-serve-somebody/.

30. "Is Your Love in Vain?" Bob Dylan, accessed July 18th, 2023, https://www.bobdylan.com/songs/your-love-vain/.

31. My phonetic rendering of Mr. DuPlooy's nickname is a poor one. It could as easily be transcribed as "Doopie."

32. Billy Joel may very well, unbeknownst to him, have modeled the figure of "John" in his famous hit "Piano Man" after Mr. DuPlooy: "And he's quick with a joke or to light up your smoke/But there's some place that he'd rather be" (Billy Joel, *Piano Man*, Columbia Records, 1973).

33. Michel Foucault, *The Birth of Biopolitics: Lectures at the Collège de France 1978–1979*, trans. Graham Burchell (New York: Picador, 2004), 36.

34. Theodor Adorno, *Negative Dialectics*, trans. E. B. Ashton (New York: Continuum, 2005), 406. For his part, Derrida proclaims it simply, but never reductively, as the "reason of the strongest."

35. Although the production and consumption of alcohol is officially banned in Iran, and has been since the Islamic Revolution of 1979, a significant section of the population partakes. It is consumed at all kinds of events, from dinners to weddings to soirées, in addition, of course, to people drinking by themselves. Because of the underground nature of alcohol production and consumption, Iranians find themselves vulnerable not only to state prosecution but also to alcohol poisoning. According to Iran's Forensic Medicine Association, in 2022, 644 people died from alcohol poisoning. See Farnaz Fassihi and Leily Nikounazar, "Alcohol Poisonings Rise in Iran, Where Bootleggers Defy a Ban," *The New York Times*, July 14, 2023, https://www.nytimes.com/2023/07/14/world/middleeast/iran-alcohol-deaths.html?smid=url-share.

36. The "revolution" of 1979 turns out to have been a false revolution, the ouster of the shah producing nothing but a new set of strictures, installing in place of Reza Pahlavi a new ruling elite that, backed by its repressive Revolutionary Guard, has proved adept at both keeping the polis in check by force and lining their own pockets.

37. Jean-Paul Sartre, "A Plea for Intellectuals," in *Between Existentialism and Marxism* (New York: William Morrow, 1976), 234. In this address to an audience in Japan, Sartre contrasts "synthetic universality" with "syncretic irrationalism"—that is, he sets the rationality (Reason) of the emergent bourgeoisie against the Christianity (the ideology of God, so to speak) of the aristocracy, which mercantile capitalism, the Reformation, and the Counter-Reformation were now in the process of undoing and surpassing. See also Thomas R. Flynn, "Sartre at One Hundred—a Man of the Nineteenth Century Addressing the Twenty-First?," *Sartre International Studies* 11, no. 1 & 2 (2005): 1–14. Flynn offers a useful commentary on Sartre's "A Plea for Intellectuals" address to a Japanese gathering (September and October 1965).

38. Sartre, "A Plea," 245.
39. Sartre, "A Plea," 257.
40. Sartre, "A Plea," 249.
41. Sartre, "A Plea," 259, original emphasis.
42. Sartre, "A Plea," 249.
43. Sartre, "A Plea," 249.
44. Sartre, "A Plea," 249.
45. More narrowly defined, *Darstellung* can be rendered as "portrayal" (*bildich*) or "representation" (*das Schildern*).
46. Sartre, "A Plea," 264.

INTERLUDE I

1. In the mid-1950s, Tabata would be among the leaders in the anti-CAD movement, the organization disenfranchised teachers founded to oppose the apartheid policy of "separate education."
2. Deleuze and Guattari, *What Is Philosophy?*, trans. Hugh Tomlinson and Graham Burchell (New York: Columbia University Press, 1994), 7.
3. Deleuze and Guattari, *What Is Philosophy?*, 7.
4. Deleuze and Guattari, *What Is Philosophy?*, 7.
5. Deleuze and Guattari, *What Is Philosophy*, 7.
6. Žižek's delineation of the process that is "short circuiting" is offered in his description of an MIT book series that Žižek edited.
7. Deleuze and Guattari, *What is Philosophy?*, 7.
8. Intuiting, again, in the spirit of Spinoza. See Endnote 2 in the "Concepts I."
9. William Shakespeare, *The Tempest*, act 1, scene 2 (New York: W.W. Norton & Company, 2019).

CONCEPTS 2

1. Augustine, *Confessions*, 32.
2. Augustine, *Confessions*, 30.
3. Augustine, *Confessions*, 31.
4. Augustine, *Confessions*, 31.
5. Augustine, *Confessions*, 31.

CHAPTER II

1. Ralph Ellison, *Invisible Man* (New York: Vintage, 1995), 581.
2. Jacques Derrida, *Monolingualism of the Other, Or, The Prosthesis of Origin* (Redwood City: Stanford, 1998), 45.
3. See "Charles W. Mills, 70, Philosopher of Race and Liberalism, Is Dead," *New York Times*, Obituaries, September 29, 2021.

4. William Wordsworth, "The World Is Too Much with Us," ed. Thomas Hutchinson (New York: Oxford University Press, 1884), 206.

5. Wordsworth, "The World Is Too Much with Us," 242.

6. William Blake, "London," Genius, accessed July 18, 2023, https://genius .com/William-blake-london-annotated.

7. Wordsworth, "The World Is Too Much with Us," 242.

8. See John Burt Foster, "'Show Me the Zulu Tolstoy': A Russian Classic between 'First' and 'Third' Worlds," in *The Slavic and East European Journal* 45, no. 2 (2001): 260–274, available at https://doi.org/10.2307/3086328.

9. Inclusion in or claims to the canon staked by women, people of color, or those outside the West, as understood by the "Killer Bs" and their ilk, not all of whom identified as conservative, were perceived as intolerable by these critics. These critics were also intolerant of the burgeoning fields of literary theory such as deconstruction, feminist theory, and Marxist literary criticism which they regarded as "politicizing" the study and enjoyment of literature. The Killer Bs were vigorously opposed by precisely those constituencies they were so determined to exclude. The culture wars consumed a lot of intellectual energy in that era, a struggle that has, as I remark, now mutated into the battle around identity, a struggle equally consuming for critics of all stripes. This new struggle, however, may have a vituperative and nasty edge that exceeds that of the culture wars in its worst moments.

10. Walt Whitman, *Leaves of Grass* (New York: Modern Library New York, 1956), 28.

11. Ngugi wa Thiongo, *Petals of Blood* (Cape Town: AfricaSouth Paperbacks, 1982), 170.

12. William Shakespeare, *Hamlet* (Oxford: At The Clarendon Press, 1965), 3.2.

13. William Shakespeare, *Julius Caesar* (New York: W.W. Norton, 2012), 3.2.

14. Rudyard Kipling, "If—"Poetry Foundation, accessed July 19, 2023, https:// www.poetryfoundation.org/poems/46473/if---.

15. Wordsworth, "The World Is Too Much with Us," 242.

16. *"Alles gut"* translates into English as "I am good." Its best rendering, however, is in the colloquial: "Everything's fine," or, "It is all good."

INTERLUDE II

1. Shakespeare, *Hamlet*, 5.1.

2. Ngugi, *Petals*, 173.

3. Learning to live in order to know how to die is the difficulty that Jacques Derrida confronts with a remarkable calm in the posthumously published *Learning to Live: The Last Interview*, trans. Pascale-Anne Braut Michael Naas (Hoboken, NJ: Melville Publishing House, 2007).

4. W.E.B. Du Bois, *The Souls of Black Folk* (Boston: Bedford Books, 1997), 38.

5. Benedetto Croce's phrase is a well-known one. (See "Benedetto Croce > Quotes > Quotable Quote," Goodreads, accessed July 19, 2023, https://www.goodreads.com/quotes/7091113-all-history-is-contemporary-history.) However, for a thoughtful critique of Croce's work as a Neapolitan thinker, see Verdicchio, Massimo, "Croce, Philosopher of Naples," in *The Legacy of Benedetto Croce: Contemporary Critical Views*, eds. Jack D'Amico, Dain A. Trafton, and Massimo Verdicchio (University of Toronto Press, 1999), 16–30.

6. Martin Heidegger, *Parmenides*, trans. André Schuwer and Richard Rojcewicz (Bloomington: Indiana, 1998), 120.

7. "Situated knowledges" is a concept that gained currency in the late 1980s because of the work of Donna Haraway, specifically Haraway's essay in which Sartre is not mentioned, "Situated Knowledges: The Science Question in Feminism and the Privilege of Partial Perspective," *Feminist Studies* 14, no. 3 (Autumn 1988): 575–599. It is, however, Sartre who outlines what this concept entails, especially as it pertains to what is often understood as the "responsibility of the intellectual."

8. Louis Althusser and Étienne Balibar, *Reading Capital*, trans. Ben Brewster (New York: Monthly Review Press, 1971), 188.

9. See *A Thousand Plateaus: Capitalism and Schizophrenia*, trans. Brian Massumi (Minneapolis: University of Minnesota Press, 2003), where Deleuze and Guattari offer perhaps their most considered thinking on intensity. There is something especially useful about their invocation of intensity in the chapter "1914: One or Several Wolves?"

10. Gilles Deleuze and Félix Guattari, *Anti-Oedipus: Capitalism and Schizophrenia*, trans. Robert Hurley, Mark Seem, and Helen R. Lane (Minneapolis: University of Minnesota Press, 2003), 109.

11. Deleuze and Guattari, *Anti*-Oedipus, 29.

CONCEPTS 3

1. In Badiou's *Ethics: An Essay on the Understanding of Evil*, trans. Peter Hallward (New York: Verso, 2001), Badiou argues for the event as being that which we only come to know in its supplementarity—that is, in its aftermath, in its having happened, in coming to know the event through its effects (the event as "supplementarity").

2. This is where I take leave, happily, of Agamben's distinction between "zoe" and "bios," "bare life" and "political life," in no small measure because of the devastating critique of Agamben that Derrida makes in the Twelfth Session of *The Beast & the Sovereign Volume I*, trans. Geoffrey Bennington (Chicago: Chicago University Press, 2009). In this session, Derrida castigates Agamben for his lack of assiduousness in his reading of Foucault.

3. I am invoking, of course, James Agee and Walker Evans's *Let Us Now Praise Famous Men* (New York: Houghton Mifflin, 2001), the Depression-era represen-

tation of three white families in the U.S. South. Evans took the photographs while Agee provided the commentary.

4. Blake, "London."

5. "Hotel California," The Eagles, *Hotel California*, Asylum Records, 1976.

6. Don Felder wrote the music.

7. Fredric Jameson, *The Political Unconscious: Narrative as a Socially Symbolic Act* (Ithaca, NY: Cornell University Press, 1981), 20.

8. "monstrous products of a monstrous society": Sartre, "A Plea," 247; "disquiet": Sartre, "A Plea," 253; "unhappy consciousness": Sartre, "A Plea," 243.

9. Shakespeare, *The Tempest*, act I, scene 2, lines 437–439.

10. Du Bois, *Souls*, 39.

11. Derrida, *Monolingualism*, 37.

12. Adorno, *Negative Dialectics*, 31.

13. In a thought-provoking and brilliant essay, Jameson argues for the importance of the dialectic without resolution. Any movement in the direction of resolution, Jameson insists, produces a new conflict—dialectic—to which we are then compelled to attend. He presents the dialectic as necessarily generative, as that which gives us to thinking the contradictions that confront us not so much again, although that too, as anew. Jameson, "An American Utopia," in *An American Utopia: Dual Power and the Universal Army*, ed. Žižek (New York: Verso, 2016).

14. Adorno, *Negative Dialectics*, 19.

15. In his stinging critique of the "technicians of knowledge," Sartre presents the bourgeois intellectual as the "most disarmed of men." This is not in any way to suggest that under apartheid, white "technicians of knowledge" were "disarmed." They were not, they were vital to the military-bureaucratic functioning of the state. They were, indeed, in the case of the state's repressive apparatus, very well "armed." However, anti-apartheid pedagogues (and this, of course, was mainly but by no means exclusively a task taken up by disenfranchised teachers), who were under considerable pressure to act in this reduced Sartrean capacity as "mere" "technicians of knowledge," in large measure refused to be so restricted and broke out of the constraints imposed on them by CAD or IAD. These teachers did not, it must be noted, aspire or incline toward the status of intellectuals, but their "disinclination" in no way minimizes the work of thinking that their teaching engendered.

16. Always the dialectician, Sartre maintains that true and false intellectuals are locked, whether they want to be or not, into a "permanent dialogue." As much as the unconscious of gratitude remained to be uncovered, as disenfranchised students we were—in one way or another, and invariably to our disadvantage—acutely aware of our white contemporaries (that is, we imagined, sometimes bitterly and perhaps more often than we wanted to, at the superiority of their physical plant).

17. Sartre's notion of "social being," which derives from his critique of bourgeois humanism, has a (largely unacknowledged) corollary in African American socio-

logical critique, as taken up by Orlando Patterson in his work *Slavery and Social Death: A Comparative Study* (Cambridge, MA: Harvard University Press, 1982).

18. Sartre, "A Plea," 237, original emphasis.

19. Sartre, "A Plea," 237.

20. Sartre, "A Plea," 239.

21. Sartre, "A Plea," 239, original emphasis.

22. George Mangakis, "Letter in a Bottle: From a Greek Prison," *The Atlantic* (October 1971), accessed November 30, 2022, https://www.theatlantic.com/mag azine/archive/1971/10/letter-in-bottle-from-a-greek-prison/633906/. In Wole Soyinka's prison memoir, *The Man Died: The Prison Notes of Wole Soyinka* (London: Rex Collings, 1976), he invokes Mangakis and writes in solidarity with his Greek counterpart; what is salient about Soyinka's turn to Mangakis is that at no point in his reflections does Soyinka remark on Mangakis's claim about Europe as the most sustainable, historic force for freedom.

23. Adorno, *Negative Dialectics*, 19.

24. "Another Brick in the Wall," Pink Floyd, *The Wall*, Columbia Records, 1979.

25. "Another Brick in the Wall," Pink Floyd.

26. "Another Brick in the Wall," Pink Floyd.

27. See Farred, *Martin Heidegger Saved My Life*.

28. Adorno, *Negative Dialectics*, 406.

29. Arthur Nortje, "Dogsbody Half-Breed," in *Dead Roots* (London: Heinemann, 1973), 105.

30. See Jacques Derrida, *Rogues: Two Essays on Reason*, trans. Pascale-Anne Brault and Michael Naas (Stanford, CA: Stanford University Press, 2005).

31. Martin Heidegger, *Parmenides*, trans. André Schuwer and Richard Rojcewicz (Bloomington: Indiana University Press, 1998), 10.

32. Heidegger, *Parmenides*, 158.

33. In this regard, Heidegger goes further in his delineation of the open: "Man in advance sees the open by dwelling within the opening and opened project of Being" (Heidegger, *Being and Time*, 159). The "open," so conceived, is always an "opening" onto Being so that Being lurks—is obstinately lodged—within every "opening." In this way, the open is best understood as the "unconcealedness [or, the unconcealing] of the unconcealed" (Heidegger, *Being and Time*, 159).

34. Heidegger, *Parmenides*, 160.

35. Adorno, *Negative Dialectics*, 406.

36. Adorno, *Negative Dialectics*, 38.

37. Hannah Arendt, *The Life of the Mind* (New York: Harcourt, 1978), 47.

38. Du Bois, *Souls*, 38.

39. Arendt, *Life*, 56.

40. Arendt, *Life*, 57.

INTERLUDE III

1. In "Violence and Metaphysics: An Essay on the Thought of Emmanuel Levinas," which opens with a reflection on the future of philosophy, Derrida provides us with a timely reminder about the constitutive inadequacy of thinking the future. Derrida writes, "Beyond the death, or dying nature, of philosophy, perhaps even because of it, thought still has a future, or even, as is said today, is still entirely to come because of what philosophy has held in store; or, more strangely still, that the future itself has a future." Derrida, *Writing and Difference*, trans. Alan Bass (Chicago: University of Chicago Press, 1978), 79.

2. Derrida, "Racism's Last Word," in *Psyche: Inventions of the Other*, vol. 1, ed. Peggy Kamuf and Elizabeth Rottenberg (Redwood: Stanford, 2007), 379.

3. Of course, such a rendering of history ties us, perhaps inexorably, to the logic of the teleological as bequeathed to us by Hegel and Marx.

4. Derrida, "Racism's Last Word," 380.

5. Adorno, *Negative Dialectics*, 408.

6. Derrida, "Racism's Last Word," 380.

7. Derrida, "Racism's Last Word," 380.

8. Derrida, *Monolingualism*, 58.

9. I have written about the phrase "thank you" in relation to an exchange between Francois Pienaar, the 1995 South African rugby captain, and Nelson Mandela, then the newly elected president, in the chapter "Thank You, in (a) Sense," in *The Burden of Over-representation*.

10. Graduated, in American terms.

11. Jacques Derrida, "At This Very Moment in This Work Here I Am," in *Psyche*, 143.

12. Derrida, "Racism's Last Word," 385.

13. Derrida, "At This Very Moment," 144.

14. Emmanuel Levinas, *Otherwise Than Being Or Beyond Essence* (Pittsburgh: Duquesne, 1998), 142.

15. Shakespeare, *Hamlet*, 3:1.

16. Adorno, *Negative Dialectics*, 29.

17. Adorno, *Negative Dialectics*, 30.

CONCEPTS 4

1. Arendt, *Life*, 47.

CHAPTER III

1. Michel Foucault, *The Use of Pleasure: Volume 2 of The History of Sexuality*, trans. Robert Hurley (New York: Vintage Books, 1985), 6.

2. During my tenure at the school (1976–1980), I can only recall three Afrikaans students who made the transition from their native tongue to English (one of whom, ironically, was a burly rugby player; another was in 9B/10B). I cannot imagine the mental effort, concentration, and discipline that such a transition—to have to learn subjects, especially in the sciences, such as physics and mathematics in your second language—must have demanded.

3. Most of Livingstone's Afrikaans first-language speakers transferred to Oaklands High School, a dual-medium institution about a twenty-minute walk away. Oaklands was by no means a shabby institution, but it was no Livingstone, and everyone knew that. To transfer from Livingstone to Oaklands was to take a step down the CAD educational food chain.

4. "Preface to *The History of Sexuality*, Volume 2," in Foucault, *Ethics: Subjectivity and Truth*, ed. Paul Rabinow, trans. Robert Hurley and others (New York: New Press, 1998), 201.

5. Heidegger, *Being and Time*, 9.

6. What was also noticeable at Livingstone was how many working-class kids from my neighborhood, Hanover Park, and the adjoining working-class community to the east, Mannenberg, who had followed the same trajectory as me and moved to Livingstone from the same primary school (Portia Primary, a middle-class school) either dropped out of high school completely and became part of the menial labor force or fell behind (meaning they failed and repeated a standard, or "grade").

7. Heidegger, *Being and Time*, 15.

8. Heidegger, *Being and Time*, 15.

9. Heidegger, *Being and Time*, 25.

10. In his essay "On the Essence of Truth," Heidegger offers yet another set of distinctions. That which is "not in accord" is "*stimm nicht*," while that which is "in accord" is "*Die Sache stimmt*"; the matter is not in accordance with what it purports to be, and this has to be kept in mind, especially when we are tempted to resort to what appears to be an obvious opposite (Heidegger, "On the Essence of Truth," 117). What Heidegger proposes is that we think in terms of "non-accordance" rather than the dialectic. Heidegger opens for us the possibility of resisting the temptation to begin our thinking with the expectation of opposites, of one thing or condition standing in a "natural" or given relation of opposition to something else; let us, if we follow Heidegger, set out to think "patience" in "non-accordance" so that we are not, a priori, disposed to have "impatience" in our minds when we offer a critique of "patience."

11. Heidegger, *Being and Time*, 22.

12. Heidegger, *Being and Time*, 27.

13. It is in this way that Heidegger insists on the study of every phenomenon in its singularity. He writes, "The *point of departure* of the analysis, the *access* to the phenomenon, and *passage through* must secure their own method. The idea of an

'originary' and 'intuitive' grasp and explication of phenomena must be opposed to the naivete of an accidental, 'immediate,' and unreflective 'beholding'" (Heidegger, *Being and Time*, 32).

14. I would like to stress that some of my middle-class Livingstone contemporaries did make their way to UWC. One of my oldest friends, Des, who is named in the acknowledgments, obtained her B.A. in Physical Education (and English) at UWC; UWC was among the only universities in the Western Cape to offer the Physical Education degree. There were at least two other Livingstonians whom I can recall who obtained their teaching qualifications from UWC, one of whom, Kimal Ravat, attended the same elementary school as I did.

15. More accurately, at UWC, students majored in "Afrikaans-Nederlands"—a study of both Afrikaans and Dutch, the colonial language from which Afrikaans derived.

16. Heidegger, "On the Essence of Truth," 128.

17. In this regard, Heidegger argues, "Being attuned, i.e., ek-sistent exposedness to beings as a whole, can be 'experienced' and 'felt' only because the 'man who experiences,' without being aware of the essence of attunement, is always engaged in being attuned in a way that discloses beings as a whole" (Heidegger, "On the Essence of Truth," 129). To think for the disclosure of beings as a whole was entirely antithetical to the entire apartheid state, to say nothing of the obstacles placed before such an undertaking by CAD strictures.

18. There was, however, also a smaller library that specialized in the sciences. Still, it was nothing compared to the facilities at UCT or its white Afrikaner cousin, the University of Stellenbosch.

19. David and Rita are now both Extraordinary Professors of the Practice at UWC. Micki, who obtained her Ph.D. from the University of KwaZulu-Natal (previously the University of Natal), has retired.

CONCEPTS 5

1. Fredric Jameson proposes this resolution as a "happy coincidence" of history that emerges out of the "temporality of synchronicity" or the "synchronicity of temporality." I offer a critique of Jameson's notion in *The Burden of Over-representation: Race, Sport, and Philosophy* (Temple University Press, 2018), 94–97.

CHAPTER IV

1. I should be clear, however. Rive was very active in the anti-apartheid sport's movement, South African Council on Sport (SACOS), which worked to unite the disenfranchise around sport by showing how the effects of apartheid manifested themselves in the everyday experience of disenfranchised athletes and the racial segregation, inferior facilities, and lack of material resources (capital not least

among them) that marked disenfranchised life. SACOS also struggled, with no small amount of success, to isolate white South African athletes internationally. Richard, himself a fine athlete (sprinter, swimmer) in his youth, was a prominent member of the provincial branch of SACOS (Western Cape Council on Sport—WEPCOS). It was, in fact, at WEPCOS meetings in the late 1970s where I first encountered him, even if we did not meet formally until a decade later. SACOS was, in many ways, the athletic wing of the Unity Movement, intellectually at least, even if in its ranks it included disenfranchised persons of many anti-apartheid ideological persuasions.

2. Unlike Rive, Brutus was a politically active writer, teacher, and sports administrator. Brutus was one of the founding members of the South African Non-Racial Olympic Committee (SANROC), which successfully worked to exclude the apartheid state from competing internationally, beginning with its exclusion from the 1964 Tokyo Olympics. Brutus was shot by the South Africa police and served sixteen months, five of them in solitary confinement, on Robben Island, the infamous prison that housed the regime's political opponents. Brutus's cell adjoined Nelson Mandela's. Exiled from South Africa in 1965, Brutus did his most effective political work in SANROC from his U.S. base—the bulk of which he spent teaching at the University of Pittsburgh. Brutus died in 2009, so he would have lived to see the worst nepotistic, corrupt practices of the ANC. That is the postapartheid political outcome against which Brutus militated, railing against the ANC's capitulation to global capital; that was a fate that Dennis Brutus did not deserve.

3. This is not to suggest that Rive's identity as a gay man was unknown within the various communities in which moved as is made clear in Shaun Viljoen's *Richard Rive: A Partial Biography* (Johannesburg, South Africa: Wits University Press, 2013). Viljoen writes movingly of the complicated ways in which Rive presented himself: "His self-parody certainly did, on rare occasions when he did not feel compelled to perform the conventional man, extend to his sexuality" (Viljoen, *Richard Rive*, 155). I had my own glimpse into Rive's private life somewhere in the early spring (October of 1988; spring in the southern hemisphere). Richard and I were talking in his study one evening when there was a phone call from a young Japanese student visiting Cape Town, staying at a hostel in the city center. Richard and I drove to collect the student and it is clear to me now that theirs was not a mere matter of student-teacher relationship that had begun on one of Richard's visits to Japan. Richard described it to me as a student whom he had met in Japan who was "interested in African literature." I left upon arriving back at Richard's house and he never mentioned the student again.

Index

Grant Farred is the author of *Long Distance Love: A Passion for Football* and *The Burden of Over-representation: Race, Sport, and Philosophy*, and the editor of *Africana Studies: Theoretical Futures* (all Temple).

Made in the USA
Middletown, DE
13 September 2024

60896069R00124